Governance Processes in Sierra Leone 1799-2014

Governance Processes in Sierra Leone 1799-2014

Abubakar Hassan Kargbo

authorHOUSE®

AuthorHouse™ UK
1663 Liberty Drive
Bloomington, IN 47403 USA
www.authorhouse.co.uk
Phone: 0800.197.4150

Published by AuthorHouse   02/11/2015

ISBN: 978-1-4969-8985-7 (sc)
ISBN: 978-1-4969-8682-5 (hc)
ISBN: 978-1-4969-8986-4 (e)

This book is dedicated to my father Alhaji Chernor Abdulai Kargbo and my Mother Rugiatu Degba Turay.

Foreword

This book is one of the governance series, which has been put together over the years in order to help postgraduate students at various universities in Sierra Leone. The series critically examines important issues in local government in Sierra Leone, starting with the colonial period and going through the post-independence era, the process of decentralisation of local governance in 2004, and to the present.

This book starts with the concept of good governance because of its importance in decentralisation and the various features that characterise it. It is followed by a literature review on decentralisation in the developing countries. What should be the proper role of Sierra Leone parliament, as the supreme organ of the state, has been given much prominence in this book; parliament's role to ensure that its activities are primarily focused on legislating pro-poor policies and the creation of a solid foundation for socio-economic and political development through coalition building is highlighted. A critical overview is also given to the Local Government Act of 2004 to give students an insight into best governance practice. The significance of decentralisation, its achievements so far, the challenges, and the way forward are extensively examined.

In this regard, I am indebted to the Ministry of Local Government and Rural Development, the Decentralisation Secretariat, and the Campaign for Good Governance. Transparency International, CIVICUS, National Electoral Commission, and my postgraduate students at Njala University have also added enormous value to this work. I was afforded the opportunity to get first-hand information from the aforementioned institutions on the subject under review, and

I was able to refine my own views through discussions with students over the years.

Although this book is relatively current, even against the dynamic nature of the decentralisation process, the need for a yearly review and update of this book cannot be stressed enough.

Preface

In 2002 a decade of civil war in Sierra Leone came to an end. Years later, the effects of this war are still felt by the loved ones of the roughly fifty thousand people who lost their lives and by the thousands of people who lost a hand, an arm, or a foot.[1] Their losses are irrevocable. The civil war also seriously damaged Sierra Leone's infrastructure and economy. This damage is not irrevocable, and economic reconstruction of Sierra Leone is under way, yet this process is very slow, and peace and prosperity continue to be fragile constructs in Sierra Leone.

As Dr Kargbo points out in this book, the reason for the tardiness of post-conflict recovery is twofold. Not only are the reconstruction needs vast, but funds for recovery have to come from donors. In response, Dr Kargbo offers constructive and long-term political solutions that will go a long way in securing peace and prosperity in Sierra Leone.

Support for and implementation of principles of good governance is key in Dr Kargbo's approach. Dr Kargbo highlights a number of principles of good governance that will be crucial when it comes to ensuring stability in Sierra Leone. As Dr Kargbo points out, good governance has to start in Sierra Leone parliament. Parliament has a crucial role in the formulation of pro-poor policies and the implementation of socio-economic development initiatives. Such focus requires that political parties in parliament, and the public at large, prioritise national interest over party parochial interests.

Despite the important role of parliament, Dr Kargbo supports decentralisation. Making people part of the political process is the one and only way to avoid political unrest and achieve peace. Dr Kargbo points at ways to revive and strengthen the traditional basic units of local government

---

[1]   L. Fofana, 'S Leone's war amputees ignored', Freetown, Sierra Leone: BBC News, 16 September 2005. Available online at http://news.bbc.co.uk/2/hi/africa/4250276.stm.

outside of Freetown: the chiefdom, headed by a paramount chief. Dr Kargbo also discusses in-depth the local councils. Since 2004, each district and major city has an elected local council which is the highest political authority. One crucial challenge these councils face, as by Dr Kargbo outlines, is their inability to generate sufficient revenue for local governance.

Another equally important principle of good governance given much attention in this book is the need to eradicate corruption, which according to the 2009 Economic Freedom Index[2] is pervasive in Sierra Leone. Indeed, Sierra Leone ranks 150th out of 179 countries in Transparency International's Corruption Perceptions Index for 2007. Widespread corruption in all branches of government is a major obstacle to foreign investments, which in turn are crucial for the post-conflict recovery process of Sierra Leone.

Michael Schulenberg, the secretary-general's executive representative for Sierra Leone, said in his briefing to the Security Council in September 2009, 'We must anticipate accidents, derailments and mistakes along this road. There are no easy benchmarks that will tell us that Sierra Leone is out of the woods.' To this he added, 'What Sierra Leone will need to succeed is time, patience, determined national leadership and continued international support.' Dr Kargbo writes in the spirit of this long-term patience and determination. He writes about democracy and peace in the broadest sense, as Spinoza meant it: not as the absence of war, but rather as a virtue, a state of mind, and a disposition for benevolence, confidence, and justice. That makes this book a worthy read not only for students and faculty of political science, social studies, and history departments, but for us all. Indeed, we all have a vested interest in stable and sustainable democracy and peace.

Dr Gerda Wever
Editor and Publisher
The Write Room and The Write Room Press

---

2   Available at http://www.heritage.org/Index/Country/SierraLeone.

Contents

CHAPTER ONE

An Introduction to Local Governance in Sierra Leone

A critical analysis of governance, the legislator, and local government in Sierra Leone first requires a critical look at the concept of democratic good governance, its significance, and its challenges in the body politic of Sierra Leone.

The notion of good governance first came up in a World Bank Report on Africa in 1989, which argued that 'underlying the litany of Africa's development problem is a crisis of governance' (Stuart and Barrow 1995, p. 427). According to the World Bank definition, good governance is the exercise of political power to manage a nation's affairs, and it includes efficient public services, an independent judiciary system, accountable administration of public funds, an independent public auditor responsible to a representative legislature, respect for the rule of law and human rights at all levels of government, a vibrant civil society, pluralistic institutional structure, a free press, and the elimination of corruption

Corbridge (1995) argues that democratic good governance has three main components or levels ranging from the most to the least inclusive: systemic, political, and administrative governance. From the systemic point of view, governance as a concept is wider than that of government, which conventionally refers to the formal institutional structure and location of authoritative decision-making in the modern state. Governance, on the other hand, refers to a looser and wider distribution of both internal and external political and economic power. Governance thus denotes the structures of political and economic relationships, as well as the rules

1

by which the productive and distributive life of society is governed. In short, it refers to a system of political and socio-economic relations – or more closely, a regime. In the political sense, however, good governance implies a state enjoying both legitimacy and authority derived from a democratic mandate and built on the traditional liberal notion of a clear separation of legislative, executive, and judicial powers. Whether presidential, parliamentary, federal, or unitary, it would normally involve a pluralist policy characterised by a freely representative legislature, subject to regular elections with the capacity at the very least to influence and check executive power and protect human rights. From an administrative point of view, good governance means an efficient, open, accountable, and audited public service which has the bureaucratic competence to help design and implement appropriate policies and to manage whatever public sector there is. It also entails an independent judicial system to uphold the law and resolve disputes arising in a largely free market economy (Corbridge, et al. 1995).

According to Brown (1998), governance is a bedrock issue in development. Development is not possible without the capacity to develop the policies and laws in order to enable a country to manage its markets and political life in an open and just way. Governance is the manner in which power is exercised in the management and development of a country's private and public sectors; the Asian Development Bank concurs (Asian Development Bank 1995). It encompasses the functioning and capability of the public sector, as well as the rules and institutions that create the framework for the conduct of both public and private business, including accountability for economic and financial performance and the regulatory frameworks relating to companies, corporations, and partnerships. In other words, governance is about the institutional environment in which citizens interact between and among themselves and with government agencies or officials.

Cheema (1998) defines governance as a set of values, policies, and institutions by which a society manages economic, political, and social processes at all levels through interaction among the government, civil society, and private sectors. It is a way in which a society achieves mutual understanding, agreement, and action. Governance comprises the mechanisms and processes through which citizens and groups articulate their interests, mediate their differences, and exercise their legal rights and obligations. Governance plays a significant role in achieving sustainable nation building and peace, especially in Sierra Leone, which was plagued by bad governance and where eleven years of war nearly led to state collapse.

Though democracy and good governance are related, they do not carry the same meaning. An elected government can operate without practicing good governance. It is only when a democratic government is anchored in good governance in all its facets that sustained socio-economic and political development will be ensured. Good governance is a means of achieving sustainable development; it helps promote poverty reduction, employment creation, environmental protection, and overall socio-economic development (Sierra Leone Human Development Report 2007).

Democratic good governance is a system of government in which those in power are responsible to the people. The present-day conception of democracy – which includes good governance – is a system that guarantees social justice, government accountability, freedom of press, freedom of ownership, institutional pluralism, and basic human rights. Democracy is fundamental to popular participation (pluralism) and is characterised by the respect for human rights, the right to form and belong to political parties and interest groups, freedom of the press, access to information, and the sharing of available resources, all with a view to eliminating poverty and deprivation. The importance of democracy in any polity cannot be overemphasised. As Budge and Keman (1993) put it, a central, democratic self-justification is that system which makes the state more responsive to the wishes of the people, and which gives them the opportunity to change rulers if they so desire. This can be done through direct or indirect democracy – the latter characterised by regular free and fair election in which the citizens can choose between competing candidates for government office – and above all the existence of a vibrant civil society. Governance is an important component part in a democracy; its absence will reduce a nation to a state of nature (a free-for-all and lawless society).

Governance is generally understood to refer to the use of political, economic, and administrative authority and resources in order to manage a nation's affairs. Good governance is the superior outcome of these mechanisms for citizens.

Principles of Good Governance

History has taught us that basic principles must be followed by the state in order for good government to become possible. These principles include the participation of citizens in the political governance process; accountability and transparency of public and elected officials (including the private sector); respect for the rule of law, human rights, and the opinion of others; an independent judiciary; the existence of a vibrant civil society and a private sector; the placement of military and security forces under civilian control; gender parity; absence of corruption, tribalism, sectionalism, cultism, and nepotism; the decentralization of political power; the prioritization of the interest of the state; efficient public service delivery; a vibrant press and free access to information; a stable currency; the mitigation of donor dependency; the building of a national economy free from exploitation; and above all good and committed leadership.

These principles are basic in the governance process, and their absence causes chaos and anarchy in various societies, including in Sierra Leone. In any political environment, both governors and the governed must ensure that good governance principles are practiced scrupulously in order for the government to be characterised by democracy, legitimacy, and good governance.

A strong economic foundation is crucial to good governance, which is complicated because a country like Sierra Leone, like most of the developing countries, is to a very large extent dependent on foreign aid to propel its economy. With the impact of globalisation on developing nations, the situation will become even more problematic. Sierra Leone continues to grapple with enormous socio-economic and political problems, and at the moment it is characterised by inadequate basic needs such as, health, food security, shelter, education, good roads, and electricity. It is to a very large extent dependent on agriculture and the importation of manufactured goods from without. It is argued that unless and until developing countries get a fair deal from the international trade environment, such as fair trade and access to markets and technology, a level international playing field democratic good governance in the developing world will remain a castle in the air.

Participation

People are at the heart of development and are the agents and the beneficiaries of development. Participation of citizens in the political process is one of the basic principles of governance because it will ensure not only a democratic society but also the legitimacy of the political system itself. The 1991 Constitution of Sierra Leone guarantees the participation of the people in the decision-making process. However, the electoral system does not give much access to minorities, which is particularly important in a multi-ethnic environment such as Sierra Leone. The electoral system of first past the post leaves the winner with all. The Sierra Leone electoral system has contributed to gender imbalance and the alienation of vulnerable groups. For example, 65 per cent of Sierra Leoneans are illiterate, and their participation can only be increased through large-scale education of Sierra Leoneans on their rights, as well as through fair representation of minorities in parliament and local councils. The Local Government Act of 2004, which brought about the decentralisation process, was meant to give access to the people to participate in their governance. However, people at the local governance level lack proper organisation. There are few vibrant civil society groups, and even fewer are complemented by a private sector that facilitates participation and thus contributes to local community development.

Respect for the Rule of Law

Respect for the rule of law is a basic principle of democratic good governance. It presupposes that the law is enforced equally, fairly, and consistently. Respect for the rule of law also means that no person is above the law. In good governance, the law is supreme.

The rule of law is also an essential factor for the effective functioning of society and the economy. For this, law enforcement agencies that effectively carry out court decisions, as well as a court administration that ensures that cases are dealt with expeditiously and at reasonable cost to the plaintiff, are essential. Legal systems may not improve without significant demand from within. Effective improvements in the justice system are closely related to other elements of participation, democracy, and good governance. For example, the development of an independent judiciary implies a watchful parliament with a functioning opposition, clearly guaranteed rights, and a constitutional framework that demarcates the powers of the executive, the legislative, and the judicial branches of government; the tenure of office of judges; and a free press which can expose injustice. Improving accessibility to and the effectiveness of a justice system of developing nations is a complex and time-consuming process because of the absence of inadequate or weak infrastructures.

The legal framework and the judicial sector are essential parts of the rule of law and are necessary to create a stable economic setting. Under the rule of law, there is recourse for arbitrary expropriation and interference. Economic actors can make commitments with confidence that their respective rights will be enforced in a consistent, fair manner. In Sierra Leone's context, some efforts have been made to improve the justice system – for example, the Justice Reform Project. However, our current justice system is badly in need of radical improvement if citizens are to enjoy equality before the law. Right now, the cost of access to justice alone is prohibitive. Because of widespread poverty, the justice system is perceived as a lucrative business.

The judicial system in Sierra Leone has been operating under difficult conditions and has gone through severe erosion of integrity and efficiency. Poor remuneration, shortage of qualified staff, deplorable service, an antiquated legal system, the lack of financial autonomy, and inadequate infrastructure have put severe constrains on the ability of the judiciary to deliver justice. Other constraints of the Sierra Leone justice system include the following:

- Lengthy delays. There are still some cases pending before high courts and courts of appeal that date back to the 1970s.[3] Section 120(16) requires judgment to be delivered within three months of the conclusion of a case. This has not been the case at any level of the Sierra Leone justice system.
- Low jurisdiction of magistrates. This problem is especially noticeable in the civil regime, where the amount in the magistrate

---

[3] A UNDP Sierra Leone Project has contributed significantly to ameliorate this situation by, among other things, recruiting more magistrates to serve all over the country.

courts should be below Le 250,000 to fall within its jurisdiction. For example, a landlord who wishes to evict a tenant who pays Le 260,000,000 as rent has to proceed to the high court because this falls outside the jurisdiction of the magistrate court. Most landlords cannot cope with the rigors and procedures of the high court and resort to unlawful means of eviction.

- Poor work conditions. The conditions under which personnel in the legal service work are very poor. This situation has led to brain drain in the judiciary system and also has fuelled the tendency towards corrupt practices on the part of certain personnel in the legal services.

Poor conditions of service permeate the judiciary in Sierra Leone. Both judges and private -attorneys pointed to the low salaries in the public sector, as opposed to the potentially unlimited amount one can earn as a private attorney, as the main reason Sierra Leone has trouble attracting sufficient numbers of qualified applicants to the bench. Conditions in the customary courts are also troubling, as there are often delays in the payment of court staff. (Sierra Leone Justice Sector and the Rule of Law: A Review by AfriMAP and Open Society Initiative for West Africa. Mohamed SumaFreetown January 2014.P.11)

- Shortage of qualified staff. The judiciary is badly in need of competent and qualified staff to facilitate the work of the judiciary through the provision of high-quality training. This is against the backdrop that most of the lawyers are in private practice where they receive adequate remuneration. It is estimated that the total number of lawyers in Sierra Leone exceeds six hundred. There are critical shortages of judges and magistrates throughout the country, particularly outside of Freetown, leading to heavy caseloads and some magistrates being forced to cover towns and districts far from their home base. All appointees for the Superior Court of Judicature must be entitled to practise law in a court of unlimited jurisdiction in civil and criminal matters in Sierra Leone, or a country with an analogous legal system. Magistrates have no particular stated requirements, and can begin hearing cases as soon as they receive qualifications to practise law in the country and complete a pupillage with a trained lawyer. There are no formal training procedures or schedules for judges after they assume office. All the magistrates and justices of the peace (JP) spoken to for this report called on the need for continuous training to be able to apply the law most effectively and promote justice. (Sierra Leone Justice Sector and the Rule of Law:A Review by AfriMAP and Open Society Initiative for West Africa. Mohamed SumaFreetown January 2014.P.11)

- Absence of law reporting. Since 1973 no law reports have been published in Sierra Leone. The importance of law reports in the development of law cannot be overemphasised. The Department for International Development (DFID) is sponsoring a project that will ensure the publication of law reports in Sierra Leone.

- Outdated laws and inequities in the area of customary law.

- Laws in Sierra Leone is a legacy of colonialism most of which continue to exist as part of the legal system in the country despite the fact that most of the laws have outlived their usefulness and need to be reformed. Since independence Sierra Leone has not successfully harmonise its dual systems of law, that of Anglo-Saxon and customary law.

- Inadequate enforcement of judicial decisions. Against the backdrop of low remuneration and conflict of interest, Executive interference and low capacity of judicial personnel are factors that have been militating aganist the effective and efficient enforcement of judicial decisions.

Predictability

A predictable legal environment with an objective, reliable, and independent judiciary is an essential factor for democratisation, good governance, and human rights. Predictability refers to the existence of laws, regulations, and policies to regulate society in a fair and consistent manner. The importance of predictability cannot be overstated because without it, the orderly existence of citizens and institutions would be impossible The protection of human rights requires a legal system capable of fulfilling fundamental requirements: the government should exercise its powers in accordance with the law, there should be an independent court system, and the system should have full constitutional rights to investigate and supervise the exercise of executive and administrative powers. Equality before the law implies equal opportunity for all people to seek redress in the courts and equality of treatment regardless of their social status. Together, these factors constitute the rule of law.

The rule of law is also an essential factor for the effective functioning of society and the economy. It requires the development of legal literacy programmes with due attention to the needs of poor and illiterate populations, as well as the identification of non-governmental groups who can effectively carry out activities to enhance awareness of the rights of the disadvantaged and their access to legal systems.

In Sierra Leone there is more to be done in order to ensure predictability, especially in the area of sensitisation of the population on the laws of the country. Even though there are one or two non-governmental organisations that offer some form of legal aid to people, this has not resulted in the desired impact on ensuring predictability. There is a need for a national institution that can give legal aid to the poor. Another area that has been lacking predictability is the area dealing with the harmonisation of the Anglo-Saxon law, and the customary law in Sierra Leone is still to be finalised.

Respect for Human Rights

Respect for the protection of basic human rights is the signpost to democracy. Universal human rights belong to all people simply because they are human beings; these rights include civil and political rights, social and economic rights, and environmental and development rights. Civil and political rights are the rights citizens have to liberty and equality[4] – for example, the freedom to act and choose what to do, and the right to participate in the political life of their community and society. Civil rights often include the right to practice religion, the right to not be assaulted or tortured, the right to not be detained without trial, and the right to a fair trial. Social and economic rights give people the opportunity to participate in the social, economic, and cultural life of the community. These rights concern people's lives and work together, and they protect the basic necessities of life such as food, shelter, health care, and cultural practices. Environmental and developmental rights recognise that people have the right to live in an environment that is clean and free from pollution, and to be protected from destruction. Development rights also include the right to cultural, political, and economic advancement; the right to have access to basic needs such as food, health care, education, and shelter; and the right of a group of people to have their culture recognised or to advance politically or economically. Human rights and fundamental freedoms (such as freedom of expression, assembly, and association) empower people to improve their living conditions and make it possible for civil society to criticise and redress unjust or inefficient state policies. A free press and access to information greatly facilitate these processes.

---

[4]   Discrimination and violence against women in Sierra Leone is widespread yet often goes unnoticed. Sierra Leone's women's rights are often denied by local cultural attitudes and customary laws.

It is argued that the office of the ombudsman has not sufficiently protected the human rights of citizens. Over the years, stories emerged in the press that reports to the office of the ombudsman about individuals who had been unlawfully dismissed were not acted upon. One reason this might be is that until comparatively recently the office of the Ombudsman was not decentralized. It is hoped that with the present decentralized office of the Ombudsman the people will have adequate access to justice. The setup of the Human Rights Commission in Sierra Leone was a timely move in the right direction.

Mutual Tolerance

Mutual tolerance is another basic principle of governance; it means tolerance of the political opposition and of ethnic and religious differences. Citizens must tolerate the views of others. Tolerance is crucial, and its absence leads to violence, which makes it difficult (if not impossible) for democracy and good governance to exist.

Sierra Leone is a multi-ethnic society that has over seventeen tribes, and therefore it has to minimise potential tribal and regional differences. Revisiting the electoral system remains crucially aimed at giving access to minority tribes so that they will not feel alienated in the body politic. It is also crucial to educate Sierra Leoneans as to the importance of tolerance, even of opposing or dissenting opinions. A joint communiqué was signed between the two major parties in Sierra Leone, the All Peoples Congress (APC) and the Sierra Leone Peoples Party (SLPP), in April 2009. In it, both parties jointly took responsibility for the consolidation of peace in the country, for advancing development, and for preventing the mistakes of the past that brought so much suffering to fellow Sierra Leoneans. The communiqué was significant because it demonstrated the political will of both parties to sit down and settle their differences in the nation's interest.

Such tolerance should be extended to the acceptance of the outcome of elections if peace, stability, and development are to become characteristic features of the body politic.

Accountability and Transparency

The accountability and transparency of state and non-state officials are basic principles of good governance and are crucial elements in the social contract between the state, government, and private sectors on the one hand and the people on the other hand. Transparency means the availability of information to the general public and clarity about government or company rules, regulations, and decisions. Accountability presupposes that the people or civil society is sovereign and that state officials are only a fiduciary power elected or appointed by the people to perform certain duties assigned to it. State officials are accountable to the people, and officials' decisions relating to governance of public affairs need to be freely discussed. Transparency in government decision making and public policy formulation and implementation reduces uncertainty and inhibits corruption among public officials. Lack of accountability has been a major problem in recent time in Sierra Leone; it has led to self-enrichment on the part of certain public officials at the expense of national development. In order for a government to be accountable and transparent, the people must be aware of what is happening in the country. A transparent government holds public meetings and allows citizens to attend. In a democracy, the press and the people can not only get information about what decisions are being made, by whom, and why, but they can also make it public. Government in 2013 adopted an act of Parliament on access to information which will go a long way to address the demands of Civil Society and the people. An Access to Information Commission has been set up to facilitate the process.

The Sierra Leone government has shown political will in both its domestic and international relations. Domestically it's done so by the creation of institutions like the office of the ombudsman, the Independent Media Commission, the Anti-Corruption Commission, the Human Rights Commission, the National Commission for Democracy, and the Procurement Commission. Internationally, Sierra Leone is also part of the Africa Peer Review Mechanism (APRM), which opens the country to the scrutiny of its member states. Sierra Leone is also adhering to the criteria set by international financial institutions such as the World Bank and IMF pertaining to financial transparency and accountability. Lastly, Sierra Leone is a country that respects international laws.

Ensuring an Independent Judiciary

According to section 120(3) of the 1991 constitution, judges, magistrates, and local court justices shall be independent, impartial, and subject only to the constitution and the law. An independent judiciary is a basic prerequisite for any democratic society and thus is a basic principle of good governance. The judiciary should provide justice for citizens and ensure that laws are obeyed; the need for an independent judiciary cannot be over emphasised. Judges have to be free to make decisions without fear of being punished or harassed. Being independent enables the courts to apply, interpret, and enforce laws, and to decide whether the actions of government are in accordance with the constitution. Magistrates and local court judges can be removed from office by the judicial and legal service commission. They can be dismissed more easily than the judges of the superior courts, whose tenure is protected in section 137(1) of the constitution. The retirement age is fixed at sixty-five years, but a judge of the superior court of judicature may continue in office after the age of sixty-five for a period not exceeding three months. A superior court judge may be dismissed for the inability to perform the functions of the office, whether arising from frailty of the body or mind or from misconduct. The dismissal can only be effected after a tribunal has recommended to the president that the judge be removed from office.

Recruitment and Career Development

In recent years the judiciary in Sierra Leone has had problems with recruitment and career development. The establishment of the law school in 1989 produced lawyers, some of whom are recruited by the law officers department; others prefer to enter private practice. It is estimated that there are over 600 lawyers in Sierra Leone by 2012. An even more serious scenario is that of judges. There are not enough judges in Sierra Leone to speed up court cases, which is why on many occasion retired judges are called upon to fill in some of the gaps.

Mitigating Corruption

Corruption has plagued Sierra Leone over the years and has had corrosive political economic effects. The fact that Sierra Leone is a poor country with weak institutions and structures makes it more important to eliminate corruption. Worldwide concern with corruption is growing in developing countries. Causes are complex and deeply seated, and they stretch along social, political, economic, and administrative systems. An effective and credible approach to working with developing countries in order to control corruption requires that it is addressed at all levels of government and business, particularly the most senior levels. Efforts need to be devoted to reducing poverty, income disparities, and underpayment of civil servants, as well as to changing cultural perceptions. Corruption control also requires effective control procedures in both donor and recipient countries to ensure probity in the conduct of business and in the use of aid funds.

Setting up the Anti-Corruption Commission by an act of parliament in 2000, and the subsequent adoption of the Anti-Corruption Act of 2008, showed the political commitment to minimise the social cost of corruption in Sierra Leone. The Anti-Corruption Commission (ACC) Act of 2008 gives the ACC the legal right to persecute people suspected of corruption. The ACC also rules that public officials have to declare their assets to the ACC.

In order to mitigate corruption, the causes of corruption should be identified. In Sierra Leone, the following issues constitute some of the identified causes of corruption:

- Poor conditions of service. Poor conditions of service, characterised by low salaries and wages over the years, contribute to corruption in Sierra Leone. Civil servants and wage earners do not get salaries and wages that ensure an average living standard. The APC government made a modest 20 per cent increase on salaries in December 2008.(State Opening of Parliament of Sierra Leone Speech of President E.B.Koroma 2008 and 2013/ respectively).

- Pressures and demands from the extended family members. As a traditional society, over two-thirds of the population of Sierra Leone is impacted by the extended family system, whereby family relations seek the help of other relations on either a permanent or temporary basis. This has impacted the public and private lives of officials or elites, who become corrupt in order to meet their obligations.

- The absence of a deterrent measure to check or deal with cases of corruption. Despite the activities of the Anti-Corruption Commission, people charged over the years with corruption have not always been prosecuted or adequately punished. However, the government has taken measures to ensure the speedy trial of people charged with corruption. The new powers given by the ACC Act of 2008 to persecute will hopefully mean a reduction in political interference in the affairs of the commission and a speedy persecution of offenders.

- Bad leadership – political, social, and religious. In some spheres of governance, there has been bad leadership and a failure of those entrusted with responsibility to provide an example of good leadership. This issue has been attributed to political patronage.

- Poverty. Sierra Leone is one of the poorest countries with a very low standard of living, reflected over the years in the United Nations Development Programme Development Index.

- Greed and selfishness. Most Sierra Leoneans do not want to share with their fellow citizens, and the gap between the lifestyles of the rich and the poor is significant.

- Ignorance. Most Sierra Leoneans are ignorant of the dangers of corruption and of the need to stamp it out. Corruption is the norm and is seen as harmless to society. There has been a tendency on the part of certain members of the public to admire and glorify those who acquired wealth from dubious means.

Related to corruption are tribalism, sectionalism, and nepotism. These issues affect the politics of any state, particularly those that are multi-ethnic, such as Sierra Leone. Politics is the activity by which differing interests within a given state are conciliated by giving them a share in political power, and so for the survival of the whole community, much more should be done in order to minimise these anti-state, anti–good governance, and negative political tendencies which have settled deep into the socio-economic and political fabric of Sierra Leone.

Ensuring Gender Parity

Fostering the participation of women and other groups who carry an unequal share of the burden of poverty is crucial to ensuring good governance. As Sierra Leone strives towards democratic governance, it must uphold the principle of equality and consider the specific interests of women and marginalised groups. Women should be allowed to participate fully in politics in order for them to share in the benefits of good governance and to have equal say in the socio-economic and political decision making of the country. Governments have been appointing women to very key positions in the country over the years, such as ministers, judges, chief justice of the Supreme Court, and head of the National Electoral Commission. The government has also adopted legislation in parliament aimed at protecting and giving more access to women to participate in the decision-making process. These include the three Gender Acts such as the Domestic Violence Act 2007, The Devolution of Estate Act 2007 and The Registration of Customary Marriage and Divorce Act 2007. There are also civil society organisations advocating for the promotion of fundamental rights of women especially in promoting the thirty percent representation of women in the decision making process, including representation to parliament. It is hoped the review of the 1991 constitution of Sierra Leone which got started in July 2013-2015 will improve the status of women in the country

Periodic Free and Fair Elections

Free and fair elections are an essential feature of functioning democracies. In order to make the formal democratic processes sustainable and to develop an authentic democratic culture, external assistance should also support broad-based and long-term development of the systems and institutions necessary for the democratic process to function in a way that is accepted by all elements in the nation. Since 2002 Sierra Leone has conducted peaceful parliamentary and presidential elections. Both elections, conducted by the National Electoral Commission, received local and international plaudit for not only the high level of transparency (particularly the 2007 and 2012 parliamentary and presidential elections) but also the peaceful nature that characterised the entire process. These were the elections held during in post-war Sierra Leone, when international peacekeeping forces had already left the country. In order to further consolidate peace through election, there will be a need to revisit the electoral system to ensure effective participation and therefore better governance.

To promote free and fair elections parliament accepted the Public Election Act in 2012

Freedom of the Press and Access to Information

The media in Sierra Leone has a crucial role to play in democratic good governance: it is an early warning system to the government and the rest of society. The role of the media in exposing bad governance without any bias remains crucial. The media has considerable power over society and beyond. Government has adopted an access to information Act in 2013. In August 2014 Parliament also passed an Act creating an Access to information Commission which will have offices in all four regions of the country. In 2000 the government set up the Independent Media Commission as a regulatory body to promote a free and pluralistic media throughout Sierra Leone.[5]

---

[5] There are over fifty newspapers and fifty radio stations, including community stations in Sierra Leone.

In promoting Freedom of the Press and Access to Information Government adopted the Freedom of Information Act in 2013. Over sixty news papers and over fifty community radio stations operate in the country without any hindrance.

Control of Security Forces

Ensuring that the security forces are put under the control of the civilian government and limiting military budgets is also a crucial governance principle. The international community has recognised the importance of peace and security for development. When military expenditure is excessive, it can result in conflict and repression, contribute to instability in the country or region, and divert scarce resources away from development needs. Civil Society and Governance institutions emphasise the importance of establishing and maintaining the primacy of the role of civilians in political and economic affairs and the significance of the private sector.

CHAPTER TWO

Decentralization

Sierra Leone's government has had a tendency to over-centralise power, which limited the effective participation of the majority of the people in the areas of social, political, and economic development. Centralization constrained and curtailed development as well as collective and individual creativity. Decentralisation can alleviate overloading of central government and can improve efficiency, equity, and participation by more people. Local participation can foster political stability, develop capacity of local decision-makers, create pressure for improved public service provision, and, by identifying local priorities, increase the efficiency and equity of resource use (Sierra Leone Human Resource Development 2007).

Decentralization is an important element in the facilitation of an active and lively civil society; it is a form of empowerment of civil society. The more decentralised a government is, the stronger the local government capacity and grassroots participation in government, and the greater the growth of civil society institutions. The Local Government Act of 2004, which paved the way for the decentralisation of Sierra Leone, will go a long way to ensuring participation of the people in their own governance.

Various Types of Decentralisation

The concept of decentralization has gone through a lot of definitions over time, and with different meanings. This is mainly so because it was thought of as a panacea to the numerous problems developing counties faced. Like any social science concept, decentralization does not carry with it a universally accepted definition. According to Auclair (2002), the concept connotes the transfer of authority and responsibility, resources, and functions from the central government to sub-national levels of government. For Stockmayer (1999), it is the transfer of decision-making processes to more directly concerned, lower levels of government and administrative authority. In order to ensure an effective, efficient, and sustainable decentralization process, transfer of functions and responsibilities is essential.

In the context of Sierra Leone, decentralization presupposes the transfer of functions, assets, and fiscal responsibilities from the central government to the nineteen local councils. Decentralization was reintroduced in 2004 to improve public service delivery and to increase political participation. It is a multifaceted concept that entails the transfer of authority and responsibility for public functions from the central government in Freetown to subordinate or quasi-independent government organizations, as well as the private sector in the nineteen local councils.

Different types of decentralization carry unique characteristics and therefore should be distinguished not only because of the policy implications involved but also to ensure conditions for success. Types of decentralization include political, administrative, fiscal, and market decentralization.

Political Decentralisation

Political decentralization is aimed at increasing opportunities for citizens and their elected representatives to participate in public decision-making process. Decisions that are made with the participation of citizens better represent the diverse interests in society compared to those made only by national political authorities. Furthermore, the selection of representatives at the local level will give citizens the opportunity to know and interact with their political representatives, which can be a barometer of sort for elected officials to know the needs and desires of their constituents. Political decentralization often requires constitutional or statutory reforms, the development of pluralistic political parties, the strengthening of legislatures, the creation of local political units, and the encouragement of effective public interest groups (Litvack 1998). Sierra Leone's Local Government Act of 2004 forms the legal basis of the decentralisation process.

Administrative Decentralisation

Administrative decentralization redistributes authority, responsibility, and financial resources for public services among different levels of government. It is the transfer of responsibility for the planning, financing, and management of certain public functions from the central government and its agencies to field units of government agencies, subordinate units or levels of government, semi-autonomous public authorities or corporations, or area-wide, regional, or functional authorities. The three major forms of administrative decentralization are deconcentration, delegation, and devolution (Litvack, Ahamed & Bird 1998).

Deconcentration. Deconcentration is often considered to be the weakest form of decentralization and is used most frequently in unitary states. It is the redistribution of decision-making authority and financial and management responsibilities among different levels of the central government. Before the re-establishment of local government in 2004, the then Freetown city council and other management committees in Sierra Leone were all cases of deconcentrated administration. It can merely shift responsibilities from central government officials in the capital city to those working in regions, provinces, or districts, or it can create strong field administration or local administrative capacity under the supervision of central government ministries (Litvack 1998).

Delegation. Delegation is a more extensive form of decentralization. Through delegation, central governments transfer responsibility for decision making and the administration of public functions to semi-autonomous organizations that are not wholly controlled by the central government but are ultimately accountable to it. Governments delegate responsibilities when they create public enterprises or corporations, housing authorities, transportation authorities, special service districts, semi-autonomous school districts, regional development corporations, or special project implementation units. In Sierra Leone, the National Power Authority and the Road Transport Authority are examples of delegated authority, and like local councils, they are established by an act of government. Usually these organizations have a great deal of discretion in decision making. They may be exempt from constraints on regular civil service personnel and may be able to charge users directly for services (Litvack 1998).

Devolution. A third type of administrative decentralization is devolution, where governments devolve functions. In other words, they transfer authority for decision making, finance, and management to quasi-autonomous units of local government with corporate status. Devolution usually transfers responsibilities for services to local city or district councils in order to raise their own revenues and to make investment decisions. In a devolved system, local councils have jurisdiction over their geographical location, and the council is the highest political authority in its location.[6] This type of administrative decentralization underlies most political decentralization.[7] In Sierra Leone, this process was phased out from

---

[6] Local Government Act 2004

[7] Jennie Litvack World Bank Decentralisation Thematic Team

2004–2008 and is enshrined in the statutory instrument Assumption of Functions of 2004.

According to theNational Decentralisation Policy of 2010 The 19 Local Councils in Sierra Leone are now the highest development and service delivery authority. Perhaps this is to mitigate any conflict between the institutions that are involved in rural administration, such as the Paramount chiefs, Members of parliament, Ministers of Government etc.

Fiscal decentralisation. Financial responsibility is one of the most critical components of decentralization. If local governments and private organizations are to carry out decentralised functions effectively, then they must have adequate of revenues either raised locally or transferred from the central government, as well as the authority to make decisions about expenditures. This has proven to be the bane of decentralization, because most local councils find it extremely difficult to raise revenue, and they depend to a large extent on central government transfer of funds

Fiscal decentralization can take many forms.

a. Self-financing or cost recovery through charging for services provided

b. Co-financing or co-production arrangements through which service providers participate in providing services and infrastructure through monetary or labour contributions

c. Expansion of local revenues through property or sales taxes, or indirect charges

d. Intergovernmental transfers that shift general revenues from taxes collected by the central government to local governments for general or specific uses

e. Authorization of municipal borrowing and the mobilization of either national or local government resources through loan guarantees

Deregulation. Deregulation reduces the legal constraints on private participation in service provision, or it allows competition among private suppliers for services that in the past had been provided by the government or by regulated monopolies. In recent years, privatization and deregulation have become more attractive alternatives to governments in developing countries. Local governments are also privatizing by contracting out service provision or administration (Litvack 1998). In places where local government institutions are embryonic or exist only at an informal level, the institutional and legal framework has to be created before any type of reform of the administration is undertaken.

The degree of local capacity determines which kinds of human-resource management strategies are feasible and desirable. Decentralization of human resource management is more likely to succeed in cases where lower-level authorities have the financial and managerial ability to set competitive compensation packages and salary levels that will attract local talent; in these cases, the advantages of allowing local governments to set hiring levels might outweigh the risk of increasing inter-regional inequalities. Where talent and skills are lacking at the local level, a unitary hiring system might be preferred to ensure that the necessary skills are present locally in all regions. In these cases where the centre retains more control over human resources, caution should be paid to ensure that the management options of local stakeholders are not curtailed.

There is fairly widespread agreement that capacity building at all government levels is an essential component of decentralization. The sequencing and priority levels of training – whether to train local or central governments first, for example – depends on the country itself, although the sub-national governments have generally been the first to be trained to accept their new responsibilities. There is less agreement on how to deliver the appropriate human resources package to the appropriate levels of government, and how to coordinate human resource management across and between levels of government. The decision to decentralise or retain central control over human resource management (recruiting, hiring, and salary setting) depends heavily on the existing degree of sub-national capacity. The suggestions above outline some general coordination mechanisms, but the specific institutional arrangements for ensuring a consistent, efficient civil service must react to the kinds of institutional changes that decentralization has brought.

The traditional approach to decentralization has been to build capacity before transferring responsibilities or revenues. This cautious method was fuelled by worries about irresponsible spending, local corruption, regional inequities, and service collapse as well as many central governments' reluctance to devolve authority. Some authors such as Bahl and Linn (1992) even argued that the lack of local capacity made decentralization ineffective and even undesirable in developing countries. The traditional approach is changing, however: increasing evidence shows that the capacities of all levels increase as decentralised service systems mature. There is a growing appreciation that management is a performance art which is better learned by doing than listening. Rondinelli (1984) reported that Indonesia, Morocco, Thailand, and Pakistan's local government capacity increased slightly but perceptibly in the years following decentralization. Devolution in Papua New Guinea has increased popular participation in government and has improved the planning, management, and coordination capacity of provincial administrators. In general, much of the evidence indicates that decentralization has increased local participation – and hence local government leverage in gaining access to national resources – and has encouraged the development of public and private planning and management skill.

The New Paradigm

Decentralization in and of itself can build local capacity. Central support can be important to maintain equity in spending across jurisdictions and ensure proper attention to training. Tendler (1997) points out that effective delivery of local services rests upon partnerships between the government and the public, private, and civil sectors. Nevertheless, capacity building should not be a supply-driven endeavour that provides the same support package to widely varying local jurisdictions. It is also not always clear that the national capacity is greater than local capacity. For example, Italians rate local government effectiveness higher than national government capacity.

Demand-Driven, Capacity-Building Programs

One way to enhance local capacity is through training and practice, and by allowing local institutions to use a portion of program funds (or their own funds) to contract for the technical expertise that they feel is appropriate. This technical help can often be found locally and be acquired quicker and cheaper than from central or regional sources. Similarly, communities (or regional groupings of communities) can be given block grants for their own capacity-building training programs; they can purchase the training they need to fill the gaps that they have identified in their own management and technical capacity. They can decide whether to buy the training from local, regional, or central institutions. When local sources are used, a local network of technical expertise develops. This local network can be tapped into more efficiently for maintenance of existing and new programs in the future. This is now the case with the capacity-building strategy of the Institutional Reform and Capacity Building Project (IRCBP) in Sierra Leone.

Empirical Review of Capacity Building and Decentralisation

Centralization is always seen to have a lot of problems (World Bank 2003; Burke, Perry & Dellinger 1999). Against the backdrop of inadequate resources and dependency on donor funding to ensure an effective decentralisation process, the service delivery element of the decentralization is fraught with problems. In Ghana, despite years of capacity building interventions in various sectors, there have been mixed results. For example, the educational sector is traditionally a very conservative and slow-to-change sector in Ghana. Support for the professional development of teachers and managers has not been effective and has not raised sector efficiency or effectiveness. The least successful capacity support has been in public sector reform, including the modernization of public expenditure management. Bank experience worldwide suggests that reform in this area is extremely difficult. There has been little success in revenue generation and almost no success in civil service reform. In Ghana, even expenditure management improvement has been unsuccessful so far after nine years effort, and public sector reform has failed despite years of effort and $15 million of IDA funding.[8]

This process of decentralization has, in the short term, resulted in the emergence of new bottlenecks. There has been little deconcentration of public services, and local governments that lack the technical support of such services remain extremely weak relative to the functions they are expected to carry out. There is an insufficient number of qualified staff, especially in the deconcentrated facilities. As of early 2003, only half the districts in Sierra Leone had an adequate number of technical staff in

---

[8] World Bank's Operations Evaluation Department (OED) for the relevance and effectiveness of World Bank support for public sector capacity building in sub-Saharan Africa over the past ten years (1995–2004).

the health sector, and in 20 per cent of those districts, health staff had less than one year of experience. About one-third of the districts lacked adequate nurses. In addition, a shortage of qualified financial management staff has also contributed to slow rates of absorption of program funds. These shortages reflect institutional and organizational weaknesses in human resource development as already noted, as well as the absence of comprehensive human resources development and management plan.[9] This is not to suggest that there are no success stories in capacity-building interventions in decentralised scenarios in the developing countries. Two successful cases of decentralization in Latin America are the widely noted case of participatory budgeting in municipal government in the city of Porto Alegre in Brazil, and the tremendous success of the post-1994 decentralization initiative in Bolivia.as a case in point.

Decentralization can be a way of improving access to services, tailoring government actions to private needs, and increasing the opportunities for state-society interactions. Decentralization can take the form of delegation of responsibility, as well as authority to field units of the same department or level or government, which is referred to as deconcentration or the devolution of authority to locally constituted units of governments or special purpose authorities. Decentralization is relative in that it describes the distribution of state resources regarding responsibility, finance, personnel, or discretionary authority between various institutional actors within the state and society. It is a complex process because it incorporates and is impacted upon by political, economic, institutional, and cultural factors.

Decentralization is a multidimensional process that defines the distribution of power and resources between state and society, between the executives and other branches of the government, and at a micro

---

[9] An independent review of World Bank support to capacity building in Africa: the case of Mali.

level between central and local governments, their field administrations, and non-governmental entities. Decentralization ensures democratic good governance characterised by:

- empowerment of the masses;
- promotion of grass-roots participation;
- conflict resolution mechanism;
- greater fiscal and political autonomy for local government;
- a more transparent and accountable approach to political management;
- ownership and involvement of citizens in local government; and
- economic development.

Despite the fact that decentralization has a high potential for socio-economic and political development, the need for adequate and proper structures cannot be over-emphasised. These structures must be complemented by sources of revenue. The latter has posed a big problem because the provincial areas of Sierra Leone lack the basic necessities of life, and not all regions have resources to adequately tax. This fact has manifested itself since the process started in 2004: the local councils have been depending both on government grants and donor support and goodwill. In order to be effective, efficient, and sustainable, the councils must explore ways and means of raising revenue to ensure facilitation of their activities.

Link between Good Governance and Democracy

All the aforementioned elements of good governance are mutually supportive and reinforcing. Important linkages exist between the features of democratisation and other aspects of participatory development and good governance, such as the rule of law and respect for human rights. Human resources development is crucial for sustainable democratisation. Also basic to democratisation is the development of a pluralist civil society with a range of institutions and associations, representing diverse interests and providing a counterweight to government. Interaction between the formal political regime and civil society contributes to and requires a responsive government, which is one of the characteristics of a functioning democracy. It is argued that there is evidence that over time, market-oriented development is conducive to bringing about responsive governments and greater pluralism.

A post-conflict environment such as Sierra Leone faces governance, economic, socio-cultural, and security challenges. Further support must be given to the democratic processes, maintaining the efficiency and accountability of public institutions, and promoting political reform and stability in a balanced way. The establishment of legitimate and participatory political systems must be promoted in the political process, and the protection of minority groups must be encouraged. Democratic dispensation, especially in post-conflict Sierra Leone, must encourage accountability, transparency, and predictability, and it must support judicial and legal reform and the promotion of justice for victims of war and violence.

A post-conflict Sierra Leone must reduce external support for conflict and prevent conflict from spilling over into neighbouring countries, through strengthening regional security initiatives such as ECOWAS and the Mano River Union. Sierra Leone must also support economic stability and economic reform in a balanced manner, through social cohesion, economic and political participation, and reintegration of refugees, ex-combatants, and displaced persons. To avoid widening socio-economic disparities, post-conflict Sierra Leone must promote equitable economic development, meet basic human needs, and reduce social exclusion by ensuring equal participation in the 'peace dividend'. Sierra Leone's natural resources must be preserved through enhancing environmental security and creating sustainable resource management systems through support for environmental rehabilitation. Socio-culturally, there should be full support for constructive social dialogue and cooperation through the promotion of a culture of inclusion, peace, and reconciliation aimed at strengthening national integration. In the area of security, a post-conflict Sierra Leone must do away with the legacy of violence by promoting individual and collective security aimed at transforming the culture of violence, which will go a long way to healing the wounds of the eleven years of civil war in Sierra Leone.

In Closing

In the 1990s, a number of factors led to renewed interest by national governments and international agencies in the local government of developing countries. These factors included globalization, economic crises, structural adjustments, decentralization, and local and domestic forces such as rapid urbanization and strengthened ethnic identities. As part of the international community, Sierra Leone was impacted by world events. Against the backdrop of the negative effects of the almost eleven years of civil war and the fact that local councils were not functional, the country decided to ensure effective governance through the decentralisation process in 2004.

Despite the fact that decentralization has a high potential for socio-economic and political development, the need for adequate and proper structures cannot be over-emphasised and must be complemented by sources of revenue. The latter has posed a big problem because the provincial areas of Sierra Leone lack the basic necessities of life and areas where revenue can be collected. Not all the regions in the decentralization process have resources that can adequately be taxed. This fact has manifested itself since the process started in 2004; the councils have been depending both on government grants and donor goodwill. In order to be effective, efficient, and sustainable, the councils must explore ways and means of raising revenue that will ensure facilitation of their activities.

CHAPTER THREE

What Is Local Government?

The Local Government Act was adopted by the parliament of Sierra Leone on 4 March 2004. The act made possible the decentralization and devolution of functions, powers, and services to local councils all over the country. This required the creation of an enabling environment that comprises a set of institutions, mechanisms, and processes through which citizens of Sierra Leone, in their various political parties and groups, can articulate their interests and needs, mediate their differences, and exercise their rights and obligations at the local level. In its bid to ensure good local governance, the Sierra Leone government should ensure citizen participation, partnerships among key actors at the local level, capacity of local actors across all sectors, and multiple flows of information, promoting the creation of institutions of accountability and the formulation and implementation of pro-poor policies.

Before 2004, Sierra Leone had district councils (now known as local councils) as part of its provincial administration; these councils became defunct in 1972 and were replaced by management committees. For over three decades, Sierra Leone was highly centralised, and political power resided in the government in Freetown. The first local council election was held on 22 May 2004, and the second election was in 2008. Local council in Sierra Leone revolves around a system of nineteen local councils:

- Five city councils (one in the Freetown municipality, known as the Freetown City Council, and one each in the provincial cities of Bo, Makeni, Koidu–New Sembehun, and Kenema).

- One municipal council (in the municipality of Bonth).
- Thirteen district councils, one in each of the twelve provincial districts and western rural districts.

There are 475 councillors in 394 electoral wards or boundaries. Although the city councils are run by mayors, district councils are chaired by chairpersons.

Some of the characteristic features of local governance in Sierra Leone are as follows:

- It is elective.
- It is multi-purpose.
- It is restricted to its own local area of jurisdiction.
- It has a clearly defined structure and is subordinated to the supreme organ of the state, the parliament.

This last aspect does not mean that the local councillors and councils are simply agents for the central government in the administration of certain services. Local councils have freedom and are local, self-government bodies.

Since the inception of the decentralization process, the local governance landscape has been characterised by numerous challenges revolving around human and material resources. Both the Ministry of Local Government and Community Development and the Decentralization Secretariat have been very proactive in the bid to ensure a viable process. Donor goodwill and support have complemented their efforts.

Local governance presupposes a sub-national government that governs through representative councils established by law to express specific powers within defined areas. The powers should give the local council substantial control over local affairs as, together with institutional and financial powers. The administrative decentralization process pursued in

Sierra Leone is that of devolution, where the central government gradually transfers power from Freetown, the administrative capital, to other parts of the country.

As of February 2009, only three ministries had fully devolved their functions to local governance bodies. The Education, Health, and Agriculture Ministries have devolved functions and assets covering services for agriculture, primary health care, primary and mid-secondary education, rural water supply, sanitation, gender, youth and sports, and fire prevention. In line with political and administrative decentralization, intensive fiscal decentralization had been embarked upon with clearly mapped-out revenue and expenditure assignments, and with room for inter-governmental fiscal transfers in accordance with section 52 of the Local Government Act of 2004.

According to the Institutional Reform and Capacity Building Project (IRCBP), the decentralisation process will go through three phases. The first phase was a preparatory stage which lasted from 2004–2005. The second phase was the take-off stage, lasting from January 2005–May 2008; this phase involved the actual devolution of powers to the local councils. The final phase started in June 2008; this phase will assess the performance of the local councils over a three-year period in terms of service delivery, and it determine whether the experiment in democratic decentralisation was feasible or will be sustained (Sierra Leone Human Development Report 2007).

The devolution process which commenced in 2005 is moving at a snail's pace and is currently facing serious challenges that threaten its proper and comprehensive implementation. To date, only 56 out of 80 functions slated to have been devolved to the Local Councils by December 2008 have been transferred to the Local Councils, and in some cases, in a questionable manner. Human resource devolution remains a big concern since personnel who are engaged to deliver devolved services are still mainly answerable to the devolving MDAs instead of the Local Councils. The delay in transferring functions to Local Councils and the quality of devolution accounts for the delay of Local Councils to effectively take over and execute service delivery responsibilities.(National Workshop on Decentralisation, 1-4 July 2013, Draft Report, Decentralisation Secretariat, Freetown, July 2013, pii)

Local Governance at the Time of Colonization

At the time of British colonization, the territory that became known as Sierra Leone had its own, albeit fragmented and rudimentary, governance structures. The governance structure was rooted in socio-economic and cultural formations of the various tribes that inhabited the area. Before colonisation many communities in what is now known as Sierra Leone had their kings and sub-chiefs, armies, people, and civil society – for example Bondo, Poro, and Gbanbanie. They also engaged in diplomacy, signed treaties, and were recognised by neighbouring societies. Their sovereignty and legitimacy is manifest in the signing of agreements between African kings and Europeans such as the Portuguese explorers and the British, who signed agreements with King Jimmy and King Tom. Chieftaincy as a mode of social and political organization is anchored in the tradition of Sierra Leoneans. The Mende political system of administration was also highly effective and was characterised by institutions and structures which, had they been left undisrupted, could have evolved gradually into viable states and a part of the international community. However, this possibility was built on sand which was washed away by the trans-Atlantic slave trade, and later by colonialism.

Native Administration System

During the period of British colonisation, the local chiefs of the various tribes of Sierra Leone became part of the British policy of indirect rule administration. These chiefs became agents of the central government under the British governor in Freetown, and the sanction of their authority shifted from the people to the colonial state. Yet the institution was meant to maintain its traditional character. Herein lies one of the most enigmatic problems of colonial history (Abraham 2003).

British colonial authorities introduced indirect rule in Sierra Leone in 1896, and the traditional authorities, such as chiefs, were organised to handle law and order. The chiefs had a responsibility to implement rules but had no power over making those rules (Sierra Leone Human Development Report 2007).

Despite the widening of the role of the chiefs to perform a small range of health, sanitation, and medical services in addition to road making, agriculture, and education in 1920, the new administration did not achieve its desired goal, even when it came to basic obligations such as maintaining law and order, collecting tax, and providing labour for public works. It was weak and oppressive, and it failed to move with modern trends such as the expansion of the market. In 1939, the Native Administration System was introduced by British administration, and its principal elements were as follows:

- Tribal authorities – meaning chief, chiefs, councillors, and men of note, elected by the people and approved by the governor – are responsible to enact by-laws and issue orders for social services and development matters. In practice, however, this was done by the chief.
- Native courts constituted hierarchically the court of the native courts, the native appeal court, and the combined courts.

- All revenues, including the chiefs' traditional revenues and a new 'chiefdom tax', were to be paid into a chiefdom treasury, and the chief accepted a fixed salary.

The treasury was to maintain a record of revenue and expenditure as well as an inventory of national administration property. The native administration did not bring about progress because the interests of the chiefs and the administration were diametrically opposed to each other. The chiefs saw the traditional system as more beneficial than the native administration, and they were therefore very reluctant to opt for the native system.

Complementing the Native Administration

The activities of the native administration had to be complemented in 1946 by an assembly. Two factors were responsible, one internal and the other external. Although internally the native administration was characterised by bad governance, the effects of World War II necessitated a fundamental change in British colonial administration in its overseas territories. In 1946, a protectorate assembly formed to articulate matters affecting the welfare of the people of the protectorate, and to advise the legislative councils (Sierra Leone Human Development Report 2007).

Local Government Administration in Sierra Leone

Local government in Sierra Leone dates back to 1799, when a royal charter granted by the British to the Sierra Leone Company made Freetown a municipality with a mayor, alderman, and sheriff. The Proclamation of the Protectorate in 1896 brought a new type of local government different from that of the colony; it was known as the indirect rule system. The protectorate was initially divided into five districts: Karene, Ronieta, Bandajuma, Panguma, and Koinadugu. Each district was placed in charge of a British district commissioner (Alie 1990). Chiefdoms were carved out of the districts and were headed by paramount chiefs. The local government system was very autocratic and geared towards absolute control of local power. Every local authority was tied to the whims and caprices of the colonial government. Chiefs were not only responsible to the district commissioner but also to the central government. The governor had power to depose a chief and appoint another, whereas the district commissioner could banish any individual. The Native Law Ordinance of 1905, which laid heavy emphasis on the role of chiefs in the government of African people, was never implemented, yet it should have been the first attempt to include chiefs into central administration. The Native Law Ordinance of 1905 proposed:

- A three-tier assembly of chiefs, including local, district, and general
- A general assembly to advise on legislature proposals affecting the protectorate

These proposals were not accepted by the district commissioners despite successful experiments in the Wonde and Yoni chiefdoms.

As more knowledge was gained about the protectorate, and as communication systems improved, especially in the north where colonial administration made some alterations in 1920, the districts were dissolved and the entire protectorate was divided into three provinces with four districts apiece. Other major reorganizations took place in the southern provinces in 1931.

In 1924, Governor Slater recommended that the protectorate be represented in the legislative council because 'the anomaly presented by the council which legislated for the protectorate having on it no direct, representative of the protectorate' (Ali, 1990). The new constitution was to make provisions for the appointment of three paramount chiefs, one from each province, to be official members of the legislative council, because under the tribal system no others would have adequate title to speak with authority.

The failure of the assemblies in the 1930s led to the adoption of a much simpler scheme. According to this new scheme, the assemblies were not to be based on tribal systems; they were held at the district level and were known as district conferences of chiefs. These conferences culminated in the establishment of district councils in 1946. By this time the colonial government had moved towards accommodating democratic local government; each chiefdom of the district was to send representatives, one being the paramount chief. Members of the district councils were to be elective, but the chiefs still dominated in the councils because most of the elected members themselves were chiefs. Each province was headed by a senior colonial officer and provincial commissioner. The three provinces had twelve district councils with paramount chiefs and official members like the district commissioner of each district, the director of education, and the agricultural officers. All of these were in turn under the authority of a chief commissioner. The post-war chief commissioner was to perform his duties to offices located in the provinces so as to ensure the most effective functioning of this machinery along lines laid down in the post-war development plans.

Related to the provincial administration was the protectorate assembly, which linked paramount chiefs (who dominated the assembly) more closely with the central government's plans for post-war development. The protectorate assembly also acted as a channel through which the concerted advice of chiefs and local notables could be on such plans.

Functions of District Councils

District councils were to perform many functions according to Cap79 of the Laws of Sierra Leone 1960.

- To promote the development of the District and the welfare of its people with funds available at its disposal
- To advise government on any matter brought before it
- To make recommendations to government on issues affecting the people of the district as a whole
- To make rules altering or modifying native customary law in the district
- To act as a commission of inquiry into local matters such as boundary disputes and complaints against chiefs

Functions of Chiefdom Councils:

- Prevent the Commission of offences in their area and assist in maintaining security;
- Prohibit or restrict illegal gambling
- Make and enforce Chiefdom bye-laws
- Hold land in trust for the people of the Chiefdoms (Paramount Chiefs are custodians of all lands in their Chiefdoms on behalf of the people and land holding families).

Reference: Local Government Act (2004) Section 28 (a)-(d)

Other responsibilities of Chiefdom Councils:

- Election of Paramount Chiefs, Section Chiefs, Town Chiefs and appointment of Chiefdom Speakers
- Collection of market dues and local tax
- Supervision of administration of Justice through the local court;
- Administration of Chiefdom finances in accordance with national policies on financial management
- Construction and maintenance of basic chiefdom administration infrastructure
- Any other responsibility that may be delegated by the District Council.

Reference: Ministry of Local Government and Community Development (2004), '*Basic concept and principles of local government, decentralization and the local government Act. 2004*', p.16

Functions of District Councils in relation to Chiefdom Councils

- Chiefdom Councils prepare their annual budgets, but District Councils have responsibility to approve the annual budget of the Chiefdom Councils and oversee the implementation of such budgets. Local Government Act (2004) Section 20 (2) (i)
- District Council has responsibility to oversee the chiefdom council in performing functions delegated to them by the local council. Section 20 (2) (h)
- District Councils are responsible for development programs and service provision within the Chiefdoms in their localities. Chiefdoms are expected to cooperate with District Councils in these development programs and service provision. Section 27

- District Councils play an oversight role of chiefdom administration. MLGCD (2004) p.16.
- Payment of precepts – the rate will be determined by consensus between the District Council, Town Council and Chiefdoms. MLGCD (2004) p.17, Local Government Act (2004) Section 58, Section 59 (3).
- 20% representation of Paramount Chiefs in a District to the District Council with voting rights, in order to project the interest of the rest of the Paramount Chiefs in the District. MLGCD (2004) p.17.
- District Councils can delegate functions to Chiefdom Councils. Local Government Act (2004) Section 21 (1).

(Ward Committee Facilitators Training Manual for Local Councils in Sierra Leone, GOSL, Ministry of Local Government and Rural Development, Freetown, April 2011, p71)

With the foregoing functions and composition, the district councils were established in 1946 and continued until the middle of 1951. At this time it had become clear that both their functions and composition had to be altered if the councils were to meet the increasing needs for modern social services and a more representative local government.-

Local Government at Independence

Local government at independence was badly in need of reforms. The SLPP Government of Sir Milton Margai suspended the district councils in 1962, but they were restored in 1966 by Sir Albert Margai – only to be suspended again by the National Reformation Council (NRC) military regime in 1967 (Abraham 2003).

The present-day local government of Sierra Leone consists of the western area and the three administrative provinces of the north, east, and south. In the western area, there is the Freetown City Council, the Rural Area Administration, and the Tribal Administration. The Freetown City Council consists of the mayor or the chairman of the municipality, town clerk, deputy town clerk, medical officer, treasurer, accountants, town engineer, chief sanitary superintendent, city bailiff, and alderman of the various wards of the city (and tribal heads).

Local government in the provinces is provided for in Cap 61 volume 1 of the laws of Sierra Leone, through the Chiefdom Administration and Local Court Act. Local government units in the provinces are the 12 district councils, 149 chiefdom councils, and 4 town councils (Sierra Leone Local Government in the Chiefdom 1991). The rationale behind the creation of local government units was to make governance effective by bringing decision making closer to the people and facilitating development in the rural areas of the country, but over the years this has failed due to numerous problems such as financial mismanagement, corruption, and political instability. By 1962 there were many complaints of corruption and mismanagement by the district councils, which led to the suspension of most of the councils. The councils were reinstituted in 1966 only to be suspended again in 1967 by a military junta (Alie 1990). One of the problems that characterised the district councils was that they did not have an independent source of income or revenue; they had to depend on precepts from chiefdom councils' grants from the central government. Precept was a percentage of the income of the chiefdom councils given to the district councils; the specific amount payable was not stipulated, was varied from district to district, and was mainly voluntary until 1954, when it was made mandatory and regulated by statute. Grants constituted the second major source of finance for district councils. The British provided the sum of five thousand pounds sterling starting in 1946 as an annual grant towards the development of the district councils; the central government gave out the money for development. When the APC government took over in 1968, it set up a local government committee and obtained international assistance to evaluate local governments in 1969. The committee reported in December 1970 that district councils had performed useful roles despite their shortcomings, but they were in need of reform. The APC government took the decision to suspend the elective aspect of local government in 1972 until reforms could be made.

Consequences of the Dissolution of District Councils in 1972

The aftermath of the dissolution of district councils negatively impacted the socio-economic and political spheres of Sierra Leone, particularly the rural communities, which constituted over 80 per cent of the population of the country. Apart from the disruption of the entire local governance structure, the 1972 decision led to:

- Bad governance
- Unemployment of rural workers
- Alienation of the rural population
- Neglect of infrastructure
- Poverty
- Health problems
- General malaise on the part of the youth population
- Massive migration from rural to urban areas, particularly to Freetown
- Inadequate basic needs
- Underdevelopment of rural areas

The over-centralization of governmental powers and functions in Freetown not only excluded the majority of Sierra Leoneans that lived in rural areas in the planning, implementation, and the management of developmental activities affecting their lives, but it also led to bad governance on a large scale. In fact, an important factor for the almost eleven years of the senseless war that started in 1991 can be attributed to the total demise of local government structures in Sierra Leone. For over three decades, Sierra Leoneans were deprived of the ability to determine who should represent them in the local councils. The government-appointed management committees were not the choice of the people. For over three decades, the majority of the Sierra Leoneans were not empowered to be part of their own governance.

The initial dissolution and suspension of district councils in 1965 and 1972, respectively, was influenced by the outcome of the report by the Public Accounts Committee of Parliament, which identified massive corruption on the part of the councils. This could also be said for the second suspension where a local government committee was set up with the support of international assistance. Despite the argument that there was a tendency on the part of the APC party leadership of President Siaka Stevens to consolidate its power through centralization in Freetown, the councils were characterised by massive mismanagement and needed reform.

The fact remains, however, that the district councils were plagued by massive corruption. Officials of the councils mismanaged funds meant for the development of the rural areas, which led to a development deficit. The necessary infrastructure, institutions, and delivery systems were not put in place because of lack of funds as a result of mismanagement. Perhaps it was against this backdrop, and also the thinking at that time on the part of African governments, that centralization was going to deliver the goods.

CHAPTER FOUR

Decentralizing Governance after 1996

After the successful 1996 presidential and parliamentary elections, the SLPP-led government pledged to continue the decentralization process in Sierra Leone. President Ahamed Tejan Kabbah created a new ministry called the Ministry of Local Government and Community Development. The rationale for the creation of this ministry was to emphasise the government's commitment to decentralization and to allowing people to be actively involved in their own governance and socio-economic and political development. The decentralization legislation and the elections meant that a devolutionised system of local government administration was in effect in Sierra Leone. This new administration was characterised by reoriented roles and responsibilities to make them more responsive to the present realities of Sierra Leone. Between June and July 1996, the SLPP government sent a seven-man delegation to the Republic of Ghana to gain insight into Ghana's decentralization process. This delegation was led by the then minister of local government and community development.

In 2002, the government of Sierra Leone adopted a comprehensive local Government Reform Capacity Building and Decentralization Programme framework. This programme aimed to:

- Devolve substantive public functions and powers from the central government of Sierra Leone to the provincial, district, and chiefdom levels in order to restore and support local democratic governing bodies, including the district, town, and chiefdom council

- Develop an integrated rural development policy framework for strategic decision making by local governing bodies
- Inform and excite the general public regarding the need for strong and participatory local governance, and to build the capacities of local administrators to discharge their duties more effectively (Sierra Leone Governance Round-Table Report 2002)

In 1997 a position paper on the reactivation of local government and decentralization in Sierra Leone, prepared by the Task Force on Local Government and Decentralization, made the following recommendations on local government in Sierra Leone:

- Regular review of local authority boundaries every five to seven years to take into account population changes
- Legal provision to enable the elevation of towns to city status when necessary or desirable
- The establishment of local authority service commission that will recruit discipline and dismiss local authority staff
- A comprehensive programme of education or sensitization nationwide in order to inform the public not only of their rights and responsibilities under the new local government system, but also of the role of local government as a service provider
- Local authority representative system wherein elections are held on a regular basis and people are involved in the decision-making process
- The achievement of a gender balance in the elections of local government councillors and in the nomination of experts and ex-officio members, including the elections of local councillors on a non-partisan basis

Legal Provision of the Sierra Leone Local Government Administration

Before the adoption of the Local Government Act in 2004, local government administration was carried out through the following legislations:

1. Freetown City Council – the Freetown Municipality Act 1973, No. 20
2. Bo Town Council – the Bo Town Council Act, cap. 20
3. Kenema, Makeni and Koidu/New Sembehun Town Council – the Township Act, cap. 295
4. Rural District Council – the Rural Area Act, cap. 75; these include rural District Councils such as Waterloo, Koya, Mountain, and York
5. Sherbro Urban District Council – the Sherbro Urban District Council Act, cap. 75
6. The Tribal Headmen in the Western Area – the Tribal Administration (Western Area) Act, cap. 78
7. The District Council Act

Local Government Reform and Decentralization

In 2000 the Sierra Leone Peoples' Party government, under President Dr Ahamed Tejan Kabbah, decided to review the local councils, starting with the appointment of management committees to the district councils, town councils, city councils, and rural district councils. The committees were assigned as a task force to oversee and facilitate the establishment of the councils as viable financial entities, leading eventually to the election of the councillors. After eleven years of civil war officially came to an end in 2002, the senior district officers, who were responsible for establishing district management recovery committees, made considerable progress.

These developments were against the backdrop of the government adopting in 2001 a Comprehensive Local Government Reform, Capacity-Building, and Decentralization Programme framework, consisting of some nine components designed to culminate into a component on local council elections. The programme had the following objectives:

- To devolve substantive public functions and powers from the central government of Sierra Leone to the provincial, district, and chiefdom level
- To restore and support local democratic governing bodies, including the district town and chiefdom councils
- To develop an integrated rural development policy framework for strategic decision making by local governing bodies
- To inform and educate the general public about the need for strong and participatory local governance
- To build capacities of local administrations to discharge their duties more effectively (Report of the Consultants on Drafting a Local Government Act 2002)

Consultations were conducted in the fourteen districts (including the western area and rural district) from March 3–31, 2003, on issues of local governance. Funds for the conduct of these consultations were jointly obtained from UNDP under the UNDP–BDP Thematic Trust for Democratic Governance 2003 under-project signed 'Sierra Leone SIL/03/M01 UNDP'. Funding support was provided by Department of International Development(DFID) as well. In addition, DFID also hired the services of international consultants from the Uganda experience in promoting local government reforms and decentralization (Task Force on Decentralization and Local Governance 2003). The objective of the district consultations was to solicit the input of the people on issues of governance, to re-establish elective bodies, and to create a communication strategy to inform, discuss, and collate recommendations for the enactment of new legislation for decentralization and local governance, and on local government elections, scheduled for October–November 2003.

Members of the new task force included the minister of local government and community development and a representative each from the following ministries: education, health, agriculture, development and economic planning, finance, and justice. There were also representatives from civil society, the paramount chief, local councils, the National Electoral Commission, a consultant to the Ministry of Local Government, a consultant to the Chiefdom Reform Project and Ministry of Presidential Affairs, and three retired civil servants experts in local government, UNDP, DFID, EU, or World Bank.

The consultations started with a formal launching in Bo, where the government emphasised its commitment to decentralization, improvement of service delivery, enhancement of democratic good governance, and the provision of political stability. The government of Sierra Leone saw the decentralization process as crucial for the enhancement of peace in Sierra Leone as well as for the improvement of the quality of life for Sierra Leoneans. The consultations centred on elections, representation, and special issues. The consultative meetings at the district level recommended the following:

- On the issue of elections, nine out of the fourteen districts of the national consultations opted for a non-partisan type of election. Three districts were tied, and only one district was in favour of a partisan type of election.
- On the question of the representation of young people between the ages of fifteen and thirty-five years, the consultation favoured special seats being assigned to this category of people.
- Special seats were also favoured for the disabled; seven districts supported this view.

- On the issue of the representation of paramount chiefs in the local council, the revealed preference was for the paramount chiefs to have ex-officio status (even with no voting rights) in the council.
- On women representation, the bulk of the participants agreed on the average that women should represent about 30 per cent of the total elected council seats.

These consultations laid the basis for the drafting of the First Local Government Act in 2002.

First Draft Local Government Act, 2002

The task force identified gaps in the draft of the Local Government Act and made recommendations for the preparation of the second draft.

The Local Government Bill of 2003 that was presented to parliament did not contain any of the critical issues of governance that were recommended during the consultative meetings facilitated by the task force. In fact, the Local Government Act of 2004 did not manifest any radical departure from the draft bill. Neither the parliamentary debate on the bill nor the recommendations of the consultative meetings had any impact on the final Local Government Act of 2004.

CHAPTER FIVE

Final Local Government Act of 2004

The final act did not specify any preference for the electoral system to be used, and neither did it specify the percentage of seats that was to be allotted to women in the district councils and local councils. In the Local Government Act of 2004, Part VI 36(1)(e), women were entitled to three positions in the Local Government Service Commission. The act did also not specify youth representation or representation of the disabled.

The Final Local Government Act of 2004 is divided into 20 parts, containing 129 sections. It has the following headings:

- ❑ Preliminary
- ❑ Establishment of Localities and Local Councils
- ❑ Composition of Local Councils and Elections of Councillors
- ❑ Meetings and Committees of Local Councils
- ❑ Functions of Local Councils and Councillors
- ❑ Staff of Local Councils and Establishment of Local Government Service Commission.
- ❑ Financial Provisions
- ❑ Property Rates
- ❑ Accounts and Audit
- ❑ Internal Audit
- ❑ Development Planning
- ❑ Bye-Laws
- ❑ Ward Committees
- ❑ Responsibilities of the Ministry

❑ Transparency, Accountability, and Participation
❑ Inter-Ministerial Committee on Decentralization
❑ Miscellaneous
❑ Transitional Provisions
❑ Regulations
❑ Repeals

Analysis of the Local Government Act of 2004

A critical study of the Local Government Act of 2004 reveals gaps in key governance issues, including the electoral system that should be used to elect councillors, representation in terms of diversity, and autonomy of the local councils. Although the 2004 Local Government Act had a transition period from 2004–2008, the end of this period has not been characterised by significant landmarks. However, both the Ministry for Local Government and the Decentralization Secretariat have been proactive in terms of its sensitisation programmes and putting in place certain procedures for the establishment of local council best practice. Steps have now gradually been taken to harmonise the contradiction between the local councils and the chiefdom administration. A Chieftaincy Act has been adopted by parliament in 2009, the staff of the chiefdom administration has now started to receive regular salaries, and all the chiefdom chairmen have been appointed. The present move on the part of the government will define not only what should be the proper role of the paramount chief but the chiefdom administration itself in the decentralisation scenario. Indeed, both the chief and the chiefdom administration are key stakeholders in the local governance process. The paramount chiefs still carry major support from their people, and against the background that any successful local governance architecture should be anchored on viable chiefdoms, the role of the paramount chief cannot therefore be overemphasised. The institution of chieftaincy has to ensure an efficient, effective, and sustainable local governance landscape in Sierra Leone. Building the capacities of chiefs may go a long way to help Sierra Leoneans appreciate the importance of democratic good governance.

According to part five of the Local Government Act of 2004, before it was changed by the Decentralisation Policy of 2010 the 19 local councils are the highest political authority in their respective localities with legislative and executive powers. These councils led by their Ward Development Committees are responsible for promoting economic development of the people and using resources and capacity to mobilise the government and its agencies, national and international organisations, and the private sector.

Little or nothing has been done since the inception of the decentralisation process to create the necessary environment to ensure the emergence of viable Ward Development Committees complemented by civil society organisations that can facilitate the process of local community development in collaboration with both government, the local councils, and local and international non-governmental organisations. This is not to say that there are no community-based organisations that collaborate with NGOs, yet their focus might not be mobilisation of resources for the socio-economic development of their respective communities, because there has not been any significant socio-economic development as of yet. Local councils, according to the act in 20(2) a–k, are responsible for the mobilisation of human and material resources for the overall development and welfare of its people. This is complemented by the promotion, support, initiation, and maintenance of programmes aimed at the progressive development of the various localities. The council is responsible for the development, improvement, and management of human settlements and the environment. Councils initiate, draw up, and execute development plans, and they also coordinate and harmonise the execution of programmes and projects undertaken by other institutions. In the area of security, council should cooperate with relevant agencies. Local councils oversee chiefdom councils in the performance of functions delegated to them, and they approve their budgets and their implementation. Local councils also determine local tax rates. In the various devolved functions, the councils will be complemented by the relevant government ministries for policy matters, provision of technical guidance, and monitoring the performance of the function of the local council: No ministry or department shall prepare any project that affects local councils without consultation; this is to avoid the imposition of projects on councils that are not in line with the development thinking of such a council and that therefore lack ownership.

Local councils can also delegate functions to the chiefdom council. Chiefdom councils will continue to perform the functions as laid out in the Chiefdom Councils Act, such as the prevention of crime, illegal gambling, making and enforcing by-laws, and holding land in trust for the people of the chiefdoms.

Local council have not been effectively creating the enabling environment for development in their respective areas because the Ward Development Committees have been dormant. They did not carry out sufficient self help development activities nor acting as a focal point in discussion of local needs and problems. These committees should have been helping to mobilise revenue and monitor development projects at the Ward level.

Since the inception of the current decentralization process, there has been less cooperation between the councils and the chiefdoms. As already discussed earlier, the Local Government Act of 2004 did not define the role of the paramount chief in the decentralisation process. However, the government has adopted the 2008 Chieftaincy Act to provide for the qualification, election, powers, functions, and removal of a person as a paramount chief or chief. Perhaps this is part of the realisation that indeed there is the need for the harmonization of the activities of both the councils and the chiefdoms aimed at fast-tracking the decentralisation process.

Part two of the act establishes that every local council shall consist of at least twelve members, including:

- a chairperson;
- local councillors elected by universal adult suffrage; and
- a number of paramount chiefs in accordance with part two of the First Schedule, selected by the local paramount chiefs.

Representation

One can only become a member of a local council as an elected councillor through a local council election, where people are allowed to vote in a free and fair environment. The interested individual can become a candidate either through a political party or as an independent. Candidates must be citizens of Sierra Leone and at least twenty-one years of age; he or she must be registered and lives in the area covered by the council and must have paid up all taxes and rates in that locality as required by law. A person cannot be elected if he or she is employed by the local council; is insane; served a sentence for fraud, dishonesty, or violence and has not received free pardon; is guilty of professional misconduct; or is a parliamentarian or member of the armed forces, police, judiciary, electoral commission, civil service, paramount chief, chiefdom speaker, or minister. The term of each local council member is four years. A councillor's seat can become vacant due to the death or misconduct of a councillor, resignation, absence of more than three consecutive meetings without permission, and failure to observe the conflict of interest rule. A councillor may appeal to the high court of Sierra Leone if aggrieved by a decision of the local council.

Councillors are the link between the chiefdom and the council. They maintain close links with the ward report all the deliberations of the council and actions taken to solving their problems, and promote the unity and communal development activities in their localities. According to the act, each local council will have a chief administrator as secretary and the head of the administration, who is appointed by the local council after consulting the commission.

The type of electoral system does not augur well for quality representation. Party politics can be very divisive, which is worsened by primordial and ethnic considerations and limited knowledge of the citizens as to what local politics for development should be. People who belong to a political party tend to see themselves as rivals of other political parties, and they may refuse to join forces with members of other parties for the good of community development. Party bosses have by and large failed to bring about compromise across party lines in order to ensure positive socio-economic development. A non-partisan electoral system will minimise this to a very large extent, because an individual who has the respect of the community will stand a better chance of becoming a good leader in the community as a whole.

The Local Government Service Commission is established by the act in part four, section thirty-five. This commission consist of eight individuals, including the chairman; a representative each from the Local Government Ministry, Public Service Commission, Establishment Secretariat; and four other persons with vast knowledge of local government, three of whom shall be women. Like all commissions, members are appointed by the president with the approval of parliament. The commission meets at least once every three months and is responsible for providing regulatory performance management and management functions to the decentralised government established under the 2004 Local Government Act.

The present act has important provisions that will enhance democratic good governance; it is geared towards open governance and the participation of the people at the chiefdom level. However, the partisan psyche that characterises the local councils elections, and thus its affairs, might act as a spoiler, particularly at the district and chiefdom levels where cooperation remains crucial if any positive development is to take place. This will affect the participation of grass-roots organizations and alienate experienced, trusted, and educated individuals, thus endangering the rationale behind the philosophy of decentralization.

Transparency and Accountability

Prior to the suspension of the elective aspect of local government in 1972, which automatically led to the demise of the district and local councils, these councils lacked transparency and accountability and were characterised by a lack of tax expenditure control, poor quality of staff, favouritism and nepotism, conflict of interest, political party interference, and absence of civic responsibility. The lack of transparency and accountability had plagued the councils as far back as in the 1960s. The then colonial government was under pressure as to whether or not district councils were to continue as organs of local government. This was against the background that year after year, audit reports turned up a depressingly consistent pattern of mismanagement and misappropriation of funds. In 1962 a parliamentary subcommittee, the Public Account Committee, was set up to look into the national accounts including those of district councils. The findings and recommendations of the Public Accounts Committee led to the suspension of district councils and replaced them with committees of management comprising of district officers and then paramount chiefs in 1962–1965 and in 1972, respectively.

Accountability and transparency of state officials are basic principles of good governance and are crucial elements in the social contract between the governments and citizens. Accountability presupposes that civil society is sovereign and that state officials are only a fiduciary power elected or appointed by the people to perform certain duties assigned to it by them for a limited period. State officials are accountable to the people to ensure and strengthen transparency, and thus decisions relating to governance of public affairs – including local governance – should be freely discussed.

Lack of accountability has been a major problem in the recent history in Sierra Leone, and it has led to the self-enrichment on the part of certain public officials at the expense of national development. Accountability must therefore be manifested in periodic renewal of the mandate of political leaders in various branches of government determined by the constitution. For a government to be accountable, the people must be aware of what is happening in terms of governance of the country. A transparent government holds public meetings and ensures that the press and the people are able to get information about what decision are being made, by whom, and why.

The 2004 act necessitates every local council to keep proper records and to prepare a financial statement every year. Local council accounts and financial statements are audited by the auditor-general every year. The auditor-general has the power to disallow any item expenditure that is contrary to the Local Government Act. Similarly, the local council chief administrator must ensure that there is accountability and transparency in the management and delivery of the local council's services.

Local councils are also subject to the Sierra Leone Public Procurement Act of 2004, which contains regulations on public procurement that must be followed by all government institutions. The Procurement Act of 2004 contains eight parts dealing with the establishment and functions of the National Public Procurement Authority, including procurement committees and procurement units, procurement proceedings, methods of procurement, complaints procedures, and disposal stores and equipment. The act gives the National Public Procurement Authority the responsibility to regulate and harmonise public procurement processes in the public service, to decentralise public procurement to procuring entities, and to promote economic development. The last point includes capacity building in the field of public procurement by ensuring value for money in public expenditures and the participation in public procurement by qualified suppliers, contractors, consultants, and other qualified providers of goods, works, and services.

According to part 2, section 1-2, the National Public Procurement Authority, which is the institution established to facilitate the procurement process in Sierra Leone, is a body corporate capable of acquiring, holding, and disposing of any property. It can sue and be sued. The authority is governed by a board consisting of a chairman, a representative of the attorney general and minister of justice, five persons appointed for their knowledge and experience in public procurement and the public service, and the chief executive. These are three-year terms, and board members are eligible for reappointment for no more than two terms.

The authority regulates and monitors public procurement in Sierra Leone and advises the government on issues relating to public procurement. Its responsibilities include the formulation of policies and standards of public procurement and the assurance of compliance on the part of all parties to procurement contracts. The authority is also responsible for assessing the operations of the public procurement processes and submitting proposals for the improvement of the processes, including the introduction of information and communications technology and the development of modalities for appropriate collaboration among procuring entities. To ensure transparency, the authority issues standard forms of contact and standard bidding documents for mandatory use by all procuring entities; publishes information on public procurement in the gazette or newspaper with wide national circulation or on radio and TV; maintains a database of suppliers, contractors, and consultants; and maintains records of prices to assist in the work of procuring entities.

The authority should send to the cabinet and parliament an annual report on the overall functioning of the procurement system, including a profile of procurement activities; this is to ensure transparency and accountability. In order to ensure the independence of the procurement entity, the act stipulates that the authority is independent. In order to ensure a level playing field and avoid conflict of interest, members of the board should not disclose interest either directly or indirectly in any matter so that they may be considered by the board. The act also makes provisions for sanctions against defaulters. The authority can investigate and suspend from procurement proceedings, suppliers, contractors, and consultants who have neglected their obligations, provided false information about their qualifications, contravened the regulations, or offered inducements referred to the Procurement Act of 2004. It can conduct, at least annually, a procurement forum bringing together public sector, private sector, and civil society and development partners in order to address issues related to public procurement.

The authority also has the power to obtain information from any party for a procurement contract, and to conduct interviews with parties for procurement contracts to ensure transparency and accountability.

The Procurement Act ensures confidentiality and prohibition of disclosure of information to avoid corruption. According to the act, a bidder must fulfil the criteria set by the procuring entity; these include professional and technical qualifications, equipment availability, past performance, after-sales service, spare parts availability, legal capacity, financial resources and conditions, professional offences, assessment by the National Revenue Authority to ascertain payment of taxes, and payment of social security contributions. To ensure transparency, the name and address of a successful bidder and the contract price shall be published by the procuring entity if the price of the contract exceeds Le 300 million in case of the procurement of goods, Le 600 million in the case of procurement of works, and Le 300 million in the case of procurement of services, as stated by the First Schedule dealing with thresholds. Unsuccessful bidders can, upon request, be informed why their bids did not go through.

Accountability and transparency is ensured by Section 32(6) of the act, which gives the right to oversight government institutions to inspect local councils' records and documents on procurement by the authority of the council, the Anti-Corruption Commission, and the auditor-general. Donor officials shall also have access, upon request, to procurement files for the purpose of audit and review.

Public officials involved in the procurement process should be impartial so as to ensure fair, competitive access to public procurement by bidders. They must always act in the public interest, avoid conflict of interests, and not commit or abet corrupt or fraudulent practices, coercion, or collusion. They must maintain confidentiality and not undertake any private procurement activities for a period of three years after departure from the procuring entity.

Since the inception of the Local Councils in 2004 there have been several court actions aganist certain councils for corruption, some Mayors were sacked from their positions.

According to section 34, bidders and suppliers shall at all times respect obligations specified in the act. Part V section 37 says that the public procurement shall be undertaken through advertised open-bid proceedings, characterised by equal access to eligible and qualified bidders, except when open-bid proceedings include a prequalification stage or a post-qualification procedure prior to the award of the contract. The act also stipulates the time and place bids should be opened, as well as their examination, evaluation, and comparison to ensure transparency and information relating to the examination, clarification, evaluation, and comparison of bids is not disclosed to anyone outside the official process. Contracts are awarded to the bidder having submitted the lowest evaluated and substantially responsive bid according to the criteria set by the bidding documents. A contract is signed between the procurement entity and the supplier within thirty days of award of the contract.

In order to ensure a transparent procurement process, a procedure for complaints is contained in part VI section 63 of the act, which gives the right to review the procurement proceedings when there is a breach of a duty.

Procurement and Local Governance

Procurement in Sierra Leone is a substantial portion of government expenditure, which makes it a critical function of the government's performance. The government budget is highly dependent (at least at present) on external aid flows. Implementing appropriate procurement reform measures may save the government of Sierra Leone an estimated amount of Le 30–40 million per year, which is why the government of Sierra Leone adopted the Procurement Act of 2004. The government expressed a commitment to bring about a reform of the public procurement procedures and policies since it assumed office in 1996, and to bring them in line with modern policies and practices in order to secure better value, reduce expenditure, and lessen corruption. It is clear that good procurement practice is an essential aspect of sound fiscal management and a basis for donor confidence. The 2004 act adopted radical measures aimed at a progressive procurement reform, which includes modernised legal and institutional framework. By 2009, in the pursuance of public management reforms to ensure transparency and accountability, procurement plans and competitive bidding have been established in forty-three Ministries, Departments and Agencies,(MDAs) in conformity with the National Procurement Act of 2004. Expenditure control has been strengthened, and the required time for processing payment vouchers and approval of withdrawal forms has been reduced to a maximum of five days. Internal audit units have gradually been established in MDAs (Presidential Speech, 9 October 2009).

The Local Government Act established councils that are democratically elected and locally responsive and accountable. The district consultations recommended that issues concerning fiscal discipline and financial probity should be highlighted, and that structures be set in place to ensure transparency and accountability. According to part 15, section 103 of the Local Government Act of 2004, every councillor appointed or assigned member of staff of a local council is subject to the Anti-Corruption Act of 2008. Section 104 requires every councillor and appointed or assigned member of staff to declare his or her assets within thirty days after assuming or leaving office.

Every local council must make an annual inventory of all council assets; revenues must be documented in receipts. There are also penalties for members of the council who commit a corruption offence: a fine of up to ten million or imprisonment of up to three years.

Paramount Chiefs and Accountability

Accountability and transparency in a decentralised Sierra Leone cannot be adequately dealt with without a critical look at the new role of the paramount chiefs in the new decentralisation arrangement. The act did not give any power to the chiefs in the local councils. Nothing is said in the Local Government Act of 2004 about their conditions of service and how the chiefdoms should be administered. The 2008 Chieftaincy Act only deals with election procedures, candidates and declaration of results, removal of paramount chiefs, chiefdom speakers and other sub-chiefs, removal of sub-chiefs, and miscellaneous. The act could have more clearly defined the role of the paramount chiefs in the decentralisation process.

For centuries chiefs have been the natural rulers of their communities, and there is no indication that the people want that institution to perish at this juncture. Yet the institution itself has been characterised by bad governance and neglect, which has led to its underdevelopment over the years. The fact that paramount chiefs play a vital role in a post-conflict Sierra Leone makes it necessary for the institution to be properly reformed and modernised. This reform must revolve around good governance, and the paramount chief should be accountable to his or her people. This presupposes popular participation, including that of women and youth.

Paramount chiefs should be well paid, literate, and aware as to what should be done for the welfare of the people. Paramount chiefs should be made accountable to the councils. Mobilization of grass-roots, which is crucial for effective participation, must be carried out by the paramount chiefs because they carry the respect of the people. In this regard, the chiefdoms should be organised and strengthened to ensure the smooth facilitation of its activities for socio-economic development, which makes it incumbent on them to fully cooperate with the Ward Committees to which the Paramount chief is also a member. The paramount chief must be apolitical – that is, he must not be partisan so that the institution will be able to serve its people without any discrimination as to party affiliation.

Weaknesses and Limitations

Local councils were suspended in 1972 in order to ensure good performance on the part of the committees of management, yet the results of the performance of the various committees were dismal. They failed woefully to deliver basic amenities to the people, including the inability to maintain health standards such as clean and safe water, collection of garbage, maintenance of the road system, running markets, provision of amusement parks, and maintaining well-planned cities and town. Very often there was a lack of transparency and accountability, particularly in the area of the finances of management committees. Corruption and inefficiency characterised most of the management committees. Political interference has partly been responsible for the failure of the management committees. They were selected by the politicians, and so they demonstrated a tendency of not having an allegiance to the people they served.

A decentralised local governance scenario will continue to face a lack of human and material resources. Since the inception of decentralisation, the process has been heavily dependent on donor funding, especially from the

World Bank. The Local Government Act for Sierra Leone envisages that each council must have financial resources and assets that are appropriate for its functions and powers. Such resources include the right to an immediate, meaningful, and consistent share of the national revenue, as well as the right to access a wide range of national financial allocations and grants. Traditionally, the sources of revenue for the councils have been greatly limited. The narrow scope of the revenue base (relying on local taxes for the provincial district, or market dues for the metropolitan areas) reduces the flexibility of the sources to provide a resilient potential for domestic resource mobilization. The need to diversify and provide financial 'deepening' therefore becomes an imperative if councils are to prove viable and sustainable (Task Force on Decentralization and Local Governance 2003). The issue of other potential sources of revenue occurred during the consultations. The consensus was that councils should explore areas of potential sources of revenue in order to augment traditional sources. It was also their view that the quantum of resource transfer by central government to local government should be increased (Task Force Decentralization and Local Government).

According to the act in section 45(1), local councils are financed from their own revenue collections, from central government grants for devolved functions, and from transfers for services delegated from government ministries. Efforts should be made by councils to collect revenues from their own sources. Local councils and chiefdoms share revenue and there is conflict as who should get more. Councils operate a bank account, invest in stocks and bonds, raise loans or obtain overdraft within Sierra Leone, and are responsible for the preparation of the budget.

According to the 2004 Local Government Act, local council revenue sources shall be comprised of:

- Precepts from local taxes
- Property rates

- Licences
- Fees and charges
- Share of mining revenues
- Interests and dividends
- Any other revenue due to the government but assigned to local councils by the minister responsible for finance by statutory instrument (part 7, section 45[4])

The central government will pay tied grants to each local council every year for the discharge of the devolved functions and towards their respective administrative costs; this was to continue till 2008. After 2008 the situation remains the same. The basis of distribution of these grants will be based on equity and reflect expenditure needs, local revenue capacity, and the financial and administrative performance of the councils. Grants will also increase to reflect inflation.

Payments shall be carried out by the ministry of finance to the local councils every month directly to the respective bank accounts of local councils. A council that is not satisfied with the distribution of any grant will appeal to the local government minister. The local government finance committee receives and considers the budgets of local councils.

The overall recommendations during the district's consultations included the need to ensure transparency and accountability in areas such as revenue collection. Checks and balances should be put in place to ensure that those handling chiefdom funds are regularly checked to make sure that the monies collected are properly utilised for the development of the chiefdom (District Level Consultation 2003). The Act on Decentralisation of local government for Sierra Leone also requires measures and regulations to ensure financial capability and transparency, asset management, and independent audits. The act also assumes that participatory government must be an essential part of Sierra Leone's decentralisation process at all levels through the establishment of councils that are democratically elected, locally responsive, and accountable. National institutions of accountability (apart from the police) have limited presence in the twelve districts. In Bo in the southern province, the Ministry of Interior, Local Government and Community Development, and the Office of the Provincial Secretary facilitated the opening of an Anti-Corruption Commission office. There are also plans to have ACC offices in other district headquarter towns (ACC Annual Report 2001), and the ACC opened an office in Makeni in November of 2008.

Decentralization, Participation, and Autonomy of Local Councils

Decentralization has widely been accepted as the only solution that will revitalise the district councils, putting an end to the bad governance that characterised these institutions and the management committees that replaced them since 1972. There is a broad acceptance that the essential causes which serve as catalysts in fuelling and sustaining the civil war in the country were bad governance and 'over-centralization', leading to the widespread collapse of state authority and the provision of essential services. The disenfranchisement and marginalization of youth, combined with massive illiteracy and lack of opportunities, accelerated the breakdown in social order (District Levels Consultations 2003). It is presumed that decentralised councils will enjoy autonomy. The act states that the primary purpose of monitoring and supervising is to enhance governance by providing capacity and support. It is not envisaged as a domineering or punitive enterprise; there must be a spirit of partnership, support, and consultation between the national government and local councils. A basic principle of the act is that councils must be given substantial autonomy and discretionary authority to decide their affairs without interference. The supervisory role of the government is therefore strictly limited to legality – that is, ensuring that councils have not exceeded the scope of their functions and have complied with legislative procedures. According to the act, the councils are to do all they can in order to improve the quality of life and combat the poverty of Sierra Leoneans. The act specifically excludes certain national functions such as defence, police, foreign affairs, fiscal affairs, and currency from the competence of local councils.

In a decentralised scenario, a government transfers some its powers to local areas to be governed by their respective local councils. In effect, the transfer of power to regional bodies or councils even in such fields as health, education, and welfare constitute a form of empowerment for the people to actively participate in governance. The transfer of power ensures participation from the bottom up, which augurs well for sustainable development. For Sierra Leone, over 80 per cent of its people live in rural areas, and so it is envisaged that decentralization will enhance political participation. Ensuring accountability will be the task of the people by ensuring that the necessary structures are put in.

In the centralised system of governance, development programmes are designed and implemented in a top-down fashion. In most cases, the local people are not consulted in terms of determining their own needs. As a result, most projects implemented under the centralised framework turned out to be 'white elephants' or last for only a very short period because the communities failed to own them and had no framework for operating and maintaining those facilities. People tend to see development initiatives as government programmes which should be run by government. In a decentralised framework such as provided for by the Local Government Act of 2004, local people are encouraged to identify their problems, prepare development plans, mobilise resources, and implement and manage those plans. In doing this, local people can see themselves as part of the process and therefore identify themselves with the initiatives, providing the necessary support to ensure that the projects succeed and are sustainable. The Rapid Results Initiative, implemented by the nineteen local councils, is an example of communities associating themselves with locally initiated projects. The projects were based on the development plans, which were prepared with substantial participation of local people, and their representatives were included in the implementation of the projects; local support during implementation was overwhelming. This is a manifestation that the community can not only participate in project implementation but also contribute towards the maintenance of those projects. The need for the activation of the Ward committees can be overemphasised in this regard. Since 2004 community development has been at a snail pace because of the failure of Ward committees to be pro active.

Despite the fact that the Local Government Act of 2004 did not include the role that should be performed by the Institutional Reform Capacity Building Project (IRCBP), which consequently did not provide for the project design to reflect the current decentralization framework, due cognizance has not been given to the decentralised structures like the local council and the ward committees. It is envisaged that the proposed decentralisation policy will take cognisance of where the act is silent. The local council is responsible for the planning and management of the development within its jurisdiction; this implies that all development activities should enjoy the support and approval of the district council. Additionally, the district council should play a very active role in the planning, implementation, and management of development projects or programmes within their jurisdiction. The local councils will provide the necessary political impetus and the required local administrative and management support to facilitate the successful implementation of the component activities.

According to sections 95 and 96 of the Local government Act 2004 consists of every Councillor elected from every Ward, a Paramount Chief of the chiefdom, not more than ten persons at least five of whom shall be women, resident in the Ward and elected by ward residents in a public meeting and a member of parliament. The ward committee is the lowest administrative unit within the local council and is responsible for coordinating development activities within the ward. The involvement of these committees in the planning, implementation, and management of project activities is very critical if socio-economic development is to effectively and efficiently take place in rural communities. Which is why there is the need to promote the reactivation of the Ward Committees so as to ensure that the ward committees play their statutory responsibility of coordinating all planning, implementation, and management of projects within their localities by bringing development to their door steps.

To ensure that council and chiefdom projects reflect the current decentralization framework, it is recommended that the following actions are considered:

- Strengthening local ownership of the councils over their respective projects by building the capacity of the Development Planning and Management Committee of the council to understand and appreciate the rationale of the project and provide the necessary oversight and monitoring support. It is also recommended that the chairperson of the Development Planning and Management Committee chairs the District Steering Committee.

- Support the ward committee to prepare micro-projects in line with the local council plan and fund these projects on the basis of an objective and transparent procedure that will ensure that the best micro-projects are selected for funding. The local council should spearhead the selection of and disbarment of funds for micro-projects.

- Build the capacities of group promoters (GPs) who have been approved by the local councils to facilitate farmer group formation and strengthening.

- Build the capacities of farmer groups to be viable and effective.

- Facilitate the use of Rapid Result Approach RRA in all group formation and strengthening activities.

To gain better understanding, appreciation, and support for the project of councils and chiefdoms from beneficiaries, it is important to prepare effective information, education, and communication programmes that will be subjected to rigorous monitoring and evaluation in order to determine the level of understanding and appreciation of the recipients.

The Role of the Ministry of Local Government and Community Development in a Decentralised Scenario in Sierra Leone

In a decentralised Sierra Leone, the Ministry of Local Government and Community Development could be likened to a mill wheel through which all the activities of local governance go to ensure efficiency, effectiveness, and sustainability. The Local Government Act of 2004 in part 14 gives the Local Government Ministry the responsibility to inspect and monitor the activities of all local councils to ensure their strict adherence to the act. The ministry has unimpeded access to all documents that are crucial to the inspection and monitoring activities of the local councils; this includes the power to enter and inspect the premises or property of any council, as well as inspect books of accounts, records, stores, and other documents. It can demand from any council the production of any document or item crucial to its findings. It can take the initiative to look into any matter or any request made by a member of the public. The ministry is empowered by the act to take action where a local council has failed to deliver. The ministry in such a case will first find out reasons for the failure, what amends could be made, the type of action or intervention necessary, and the type of support or capacity building that such a council might need to strengthen its management. The ministry is empowered by law to reduce or withhold grants or funds for any council that fails or refuses to rectify a default within ninety days. In case of a dispute, the ministry will find an amicable solution between and among the disputants; this could be between local councils, a council and the ministry or other agency, or a council and a national organisation. If the ministry cannot solve the dispute, it will report the matter and make recommendation to the Inter-Ministerial Committee on Local Government and Decentralization.

The Inter-Ministerial Committee has been created by the Local Government Act to complement the activities of the Ministry of Local Government and Community Development. It consists of the vice president of the Republic of Sierra Leone (who is the chairperson); the ministers of local government, finance, development and economic planning, education, and health and sanitation, agriculture, and works; the attorney-general; and four chairpersons of local councils. The Committee on Local Government and Decentralization focuses on proper implementation of the act; oversees the activities of the local councils and how they could be made effective, efficient, and sustainable, ensuring democratic good governance; and arbitrates disputes between ministries, departments and agencies of government, provincial administrations, and local councils.

The act has given enormous powers to the ministry. For example, section 99(1) gives the ministry the power to approve agreements involving both local and international actors. The fear, however, is that because the Local Government Act of 2004 makes for a partisan type of elections, the ruling party might use its leverage with other parties to marginalise those councils under the control of other party or parties.

CHAPTER SIX

Reintroduction of District Officers

The overarching aim of the local government administration in Sierra Leone, as articulated by the Local Government Act of 2004, is ensuring democratic good governance characterised by efficient service delivery, accountability and transparency, and local participation in the decision making and development processes. Since 2004 when the act was enacted, the decentralisation process has faced numerous challenges.

The aim of the research is to take a very critical look at the reintroduction of the district officers and their impact on the decentralisation process. The research is anchored on the following objectives:

- to examine the governance implications and challenges of the reintroducing of the district officers to the local governance administration:
- to critically assess the possible role/contribution of district officers in a decentralised governance environment in Sierra Leone;
- to critically analyse current debate by both government and the opposition on the issue of reintroduction of district officers;
- to recommend as to what should be the proper role of the district officers aimed at enhancing democratic good governance, particularly in order to bridge the divide between the local council and the chiefdom administrations; and
- to advance and defend the thesis that the role of district officers should be seen in transition and that ultimate responsibility of chiefdom administration should be with the local councils.

Why Decentralisation?

According to Karingi in his paper titled *Theoretical and Practical Issues in Decentralisation and Fiscal Devolution: Lesions from and for Kenya,* decentralisation could be seen by democrats as a way of increasing responsiveness of the government to the demands of individual citizens, to the extent that one of the most compelling motivations for decentralisation is the strong correlation thought to exist between decentralisation and democracy. Decentralisation is therefore seen to promote such values as equality, responsiveness, and accountability; in the liberal democratic tradition, it is believed that more responsive and accountable local governments would contribute to this form of national democracy (Njuguna 2003, p.1).

Ian Scott sees decentralisation" as a cure for cumbersome decision, making it at the centre a means of achieving greater popular participation and empowering local communities, an aid to planning improved policy implementation and more effective delivery of services, a way of generating additional resources, and at its widest a necessary pre-condition for small-scale, ecologically sustainable development (Scott 1996, p. 3).

Type of Decentralization

There are four popular forms of decentralisation: deconcentration, delegation, devolution, and privatisation. Sierra Leone has adopted the devolution method in its decentralisation process. The devolution process is also known as political or democratic decentralisation; this process entails the transfer of power from the higher levels of the central government to the local councils in the periphery. This means that the parliament of Sierra Leone, in enacting the Local Government Act of 2004, has devolved power to the nineteen local councils that constitute the elected representatives of the people. The rationale here is that the local councils are the representative bodies of the people, are democratically elected, and are in a better position to secure and promote the local community interest to the fullest. This is the core logic argument for decentralisation. The fact remains that local government administration in Sierra Leone constitutes the representatives of individuals in their respective regions who are resident within their jurisdictions and are not only better placed in terms of information and the needs and preferences of their respective communities, but are also able to respond more effectively in order to satisfy their needs.

Provisions of the Local Government Act of 2004

There is no provision for district officers in both the Local Government Act of 2004 (LG 2004) and the Chieftaincy Act of 2008 to be part of the local governance administration process. According to LG 2004, the districts now have local and town councils, and the local councils constitute the highest political authority. Each local council has a chief administrator who acts as secretary to the council and the head of administration of the local council.

The relationship between the councils and chiefdoms is contained in part V of the LG 2004: section 20(h-j) deals with local council supervision of the chiefdom councils in the performance of functions delegated to them by the local councils, approval of the budgets of chiefdom councils, and supervising the implementation of such budgets and the performance of devolved functions that are listed in the third schedule. These functions include all the functions of government ministries and agencies. The chiefdom councils are required by LG 2004 to submit quarterly reports reflecting financial matters on the delegated function. The relevant ministry will be responsible for policy matters, the provision of technical guidance to the local councils, and the monitoring of performance of the functions of the local councils.

Both the local councils and the chiefdom councils also share revenue, determination of the tax by the council, the sharing of mining revenue, and the issuing of licence. According to section 27, chiefdom councils shall cooperate with local councils in the performance of the functions of the local councils. Such cooperation does not preclude the chiefdom councils performing the functions provided for in the Chiefdom Councils Act; these include the prevention of crime, the prohibition or restriction of gambling, making and enforcing of by-laws, and holding land in trust of the people of the chiefdoms.

The act does not contain any provision indicating that the chiefdom councils are subordinate institutions to the local councils. The chiefdom councils are only requested to cooperate with the local councils in the performance of the functions of the local councils. The fact remains that the chiefdoms constitute a separate entity of their own regulated by other legislations, including the Chiefdom Act and the Provinces Act. The question remains as to whether the chiefdoms should be administered separately from the local council administration, because it is argued that it is inconceivable for local council's administration to operate without the administrative control of the chiefdoms. The environment or the operational area of the local councils is the chiefdom and constitutes a very crucial recipient of the socio-economic and political outcomes of the activities of the local council administration.

It is argued that the failure of LG 2004 to incorporate the administration of the chiefdoms was perhaps due to the fact that at that time, government lacked the capacity to do so. What perhaps was seen as urgent was the decentralisation process that was going to bring some form of relief to the burden of the central government, even after the eleven years of war. Decentralisation was also seen by both international partners and the government of Sierra Leone as a step to facilitate the post-conflict reconstruction and developmental process. That was perhaps why much premium was not given to the incorporation of provincial administration with in a decentralised scenario.

It is argued that the lacuna between the council and chiefdom was foreseeable because past local government administration pointed to that fact. Perhaps it is this gap that has become so glaring that the Ministry of Local Government has decided to reintroduce the district officers (Dos). If it is accepted that the DOs have a crucial role to play in the current decentralisation process, will it be wise to accept all the traditional functions and powers of both the provincial secretary and the district officer wholesale into the new decentralisation administration? It is argued that the government should carry out further research with a view to modernising the local government administration by taking a very critical look of the Local Government Act of 2004 and effect the necessary amendment.

District Officers and the Decentralisation Process

The impact of the reintroduction of the DOs on democratic good governance that should characterise local councils is of grave concern to many. It is argued that there are possible governance implications and challenges that will impact the decentralisation process as a result of the reintroducing of the DOs – among other things, the overlapping of functions between the chief administrator, the head of the local councils, administration, and political interference on the part of the government of the day. The allegiance of the paramount chiefs is also problematic: will they imbibe good governance values by being impartial or will they support the government of the day? What about the policies of the Ministry of Local Government that tended to contradict those of local councils, particularly in councils controlled by the opposition? These and more are some of the possible conjectures in a decentralisation scenario where both local councils and chiefdom administrations are carried out by different institution with different ideologies.

It is argued that the reintroduction of the DOs has its legal basis from section 154(2) of the Sierra Leone Constitution, which has a provision for a provincial secretary that presupposes the existence of DOs who are under the supervision of the former. The Provinces Act of 1965 (28) talks in detail about the functions of the provincial secretary and the district officers, which were not repealed or incorporated by LG 2004.

It is argued that the reintroduction of the DOs is inevitable because the present functions of the local councils do not include the following, which before now had been the purview of the DOs.

- Chieftaincy matters
- Land matters
- Bush disputes
- Boundary disputes
- Secret societies
- Traditional disputes and issues

It has been argued that the above issues are outside the purview of the political jurisdiction of the local council administration, and such issues could only perhaps be properly handle by the provincial secretary's representative in the person of the DOs. It is argued also that the absence of the DOs has been negatively impacting the review of the local court appeal cases – which have been transferred to the magistrate courts, which are overburdened with criminal cases, causing an undue delay of justice. It is argued that the DOs should be adequately empowered with customary law officers to review both the customary and civil cases from the local courts – a situation the local council will not contend with at the moment.

Another argument put forward for the reintroduction of the DOs is that they could serve as connecting rods between the councils and the chiefdoms where the paramount chief is head. The DOs are civil servants and are therefore seen as apolitical; such a situation will help to ensure cooperation between and among political parties. It is argued that chiefs are more at ease with DOs than politicians, and the latter will checkmate the power of paramount chiefs. Non-governmental organisations, businesspeople, and other non-political stakeholders will easily confide in the DOs far more than the political chairman.

It is argued that despite the aptness of the role of the DOs in the present decentralisation process, their traditional functions should be critically examine with a view to ensuring democratic good governance in provincial administration. It has been argued by the opposition that the reintroduction of the DOs will, to a very large extent, lead to political interference on the part of any government in power in local council administration. This is an issue that should be looked at critically even against the backdrop that the DOs are not only civil servants but must also be politically neutral and therefore should play the political chess game with a high degree of independence. It has been argued the civil servants over the years have allowed themselves to be politicised, which has impacted and continue to impact the governance process negatively.

Given the aptness of the district officers as having a role to play in the decentralisation process, they will have a Herculean task to perform in the chiefdoms. Presently it is argued that chiefdoms councils lack capacity. An important task is to ensure the building of that capacity both human and material, even that of the provincial secretary. More provincial secretaries should be recruited to reduce the burden of work they have to carry at the moment. In all five districts in the northern province of the country, there is only one provincial secretary to serve the whole area, which is very vast. In this regard it has been argued that the budget for provincial administration be increased to ensure effectiveness and efficiency, if the provincial administration is to positively impact the decentralisation process. DOs should ensure that they translate their neutrality by ensuring that the paramount chiefs become non partisan viz-a-vis the government of the day It could be argued that the success of the DOs in enhancing the relationship between the local councils and chiefdoms will depend on their neutrality and impartiality relating to the political environment of the respect regions. The terms of reference of the DOs should be clear cut so as not to conflict the functions of the chief administrator of the local councils. The fact remains that the chief administrator's position is at the level of a permanent secretary, whereas the DOs are at the level of a cadet administrator. Local councils should not be answerable to DOs.

It is argued that the paramount chiefs prefer to be answerable to the DOs rather than to the chief administrator, and so it should be the task of the DOs to instil good governance culture in them. It has been argued that there is a tendency for paramount chiefs wanting to live beyond their means, and in that regard they tend to exploit their people. It is also argued that the performance of the paramount chiefs is very low despite the fact that over 50 per cent of chiefs are graduates of various universities both home and overseas and have served central government administration. There is a tendency also for paramount chiefs not to reside in their respective chiefdoms.

The reintroduction of the district officers into the present decentralisation process in Sierra Leone in July 2010 has provoked very heated debate as to whether its introduction will jeopardise the heavily challenged decentralization process.

Arguments for Reintroduction

According to the government of Sierra Leone, the introduction of the district officers in each of the twelve districts would ensure close collaboration between the district and the government. The minister of local government said that the reintroduction of the DOs was to ensure the dissemination of government information in a timely manner, as well as create the avenue for settling disputes, monitoring the activities of non-governmental organisations, relating more closely with government agencies, and ensuring that paramount chiefs do not abuse power. He emphasised that district officers were delegated staff of the central government (Ministry of Local Government), part of the provincial administration, and directly supervised by the provincial secretary.

District commissioners existed as part of the British Local Government Administration in Sierra Leone during the colonial era and were responsible for the collection of tax, the construction of schools, and other public facilities.

Arguments against Reintroduction

According to a 30 July 2010 article on the SLPP website, captioned 'SLPP MP Condemns Reintroduction of District Officers in Sierra Leone', the SLPP party views the decision to bring back district officers by the All Peoples Congress (the party in power) as having a political and retrogressive psyche. The SLPP believes that the tactic is aimed at undermining and reversing the decentralisation process in Sierra Leone, and it argues that the responsibilities of Dos will surely overlap with that of the chief administrators at the local councils. With the DOs accountable only to the central government, there will be conflict between the district officers and the local council administration. The article added that the reintroduction will create chaos and confusion in the district council administration. The SLPP holds the position that the APC government is disturbed by the fact that it does not have absolute control of all districts, and that despite the fact that it is in charge of central government, it can only influence ten out of nineteen local councils (http://news.sl/drwebsite/publish/article_pp.5-7).

Possible Role of DOs in the New Governance Dispensation

It could be argued that the reintroduction of DOs is apt because of the non-existence of provisions in the Local Government Act of 2004 that are aimed at the integration of chiefdoms in to the Local Council Administration. The fact that LG 2004 did not take over the administration of chiefdoms gives the introduction of DOs more credence; their reintroduction will ensure sanity in the chiefdoms which are, to a very large extent, not only disconnected from the local councils but also disorganised socio-economically. It could be argued that if the Office of the Provincial Secretary is adequately capacitated, such as the recruitment of more provincial secretaries and adequate funding, this will facilitate the functions of the provincial secretary and that of the DOs as enshrined in the Provinces Act of 1965. Perhaps in order to ensure a new good governance dispensation, the DOs should be seen as performing a transitional function until such a time when the local councils' administration are capable of taking over the control of the administration of the chiefdoms. It is inconceivable for local councils to become effective, efficient, and sustainable without having control of the chiefdoms. Local councils are elected representatives of the people who live in no other geographical area but the chiefdoms. Thus if the chiefdoms are characterised by a different administration where local council administration only has the role to oversee or monitor local council projects, there might be the possibility of conflicts between the respective administrations. Such a situation, it is argued, will not bode well for ensuring an effective, efficient, and sustainable decentralisation process anchored on democratic good governance.

Present Status of Chiefdom Governance

The newly appointed district officers will have to contend with 149 chiefdoms headed by paramount chiefs. These chiefdoms, it is argued, are to a very large extent not properly organised, and they lack good governance, basic amenities, and crucial institutions and structures that would positively complement the local council administration in the bid to ensuring socio-economic and political development. The majority of the people in these regions are very poor and could not afford even a dollar (4000 Leones) a day.

The chiefdom has been highly dependent on government grants, however the government of the All Peoples' Congress Party has decided to ensure the payment of the paramount chiefs and their chiefdom officials who have not been paid for decades. This assurance was translated into reality in the 2014 financial year Supplementary Government Budget presented to parliament by the finance minister who said "The implementation of this policy has resulted in an increase in the wage bill by Le.13.4 billion(Statement on the Supplementary Government Budget for Financial Year 2014.10th July 2014 Tower Hill Freetown, p3). The chiefdoms have been requested to decide on the utilisation of the revenue it collected for 2008–2009, which totalled Le 5 billion, excluding a government grant of Le 946 million. The move by the government to initially impose a temporary ban on the use of the funds was to ensure that sanity was established in the chiefdoms for transparency and accountability, and as part of chiefdom reform, court chairmen were installed all over the country. Parliament enacted a 2009 Chieftaincy Act to provide for the qualification, election, powers, functions, and removal of a person as a paramount chief, and for other matters connected with chieftaincy. It is argued that the core of this reform should find a place for the paramount chiefs by integrating that institution into the governance process. This perhaps will go a long way to giving the institution of chieftaincy something to play with rather than becoming spoilers of the process that bring about democratic good governance in the local administration system.

It is argued that since the decentralisation process started in 2004, the chiefdoms have not felt the positive impact of the process. Chiefdoms perceive the decentralisation drive as 'decentralised, but centralised'. This is because while the national government has devolved some of its powers, functions, and services to the local councils, the chiefdoms were not given any defined role in LG 2004. It was only comparatively recently that a serious attempt has been made to ensure the payment of officials of chiefdom administration after over a decade of benign neglect of a crucial institution of governance. The government has also installed all the 288 court chairmen in all the chiefdoms with the payment of salary. Elections have been held to fill thirty-eight paramount chief vacancies, and comparatively recently the reintroduction of DOs was aimed at bringing about better governance and socio-economic development at the chiefdom level. It could be argued that such an environment will no doubt minimise the tendency on the part of the paramount chiefs treating their chiefdoms as personal fiefdoms, but they will also start to see themselves as custodians of the rights of their people.

Conclusion

An attempt has been made to critically examine the governance implications and challenges as a result of reintroducing district officers against the background of the current decentralisation process. It has been identified that the Local Government Act of 2004 did not have adequate provisions that would have made the district offices irrelevant or a spent force in our local governance administration in Sierra Leone. It is an irrefutable fact that there has been a lacuna between the local councils and chiefdoms which must be bridged in order to ensure the proper integration of the chiefdoms for better governance.

It is therefore argued that the reintroduction of DOs is apt and even timely six years after the inception of the decentralisation process in Sierra Leone. What is crucial, however, is to ensure that the Dos' terms of reference not only are in conflict with that of the chief administrator in the local councils, but also reflect the changed situation of the country, specifically that of a people who has shed the colonial mentality to that of a psyche characterised by democratic good governance. Indeed, DOs can play a very crucial role in the current decentralisation process by becoming intermediaries between and among all the stakeholders, including political parties, local governance institutions, and the chiefdoms on the one hand, and the provincial administration and government on the other. Such a role, it has been emphasised by many, must be performed with absolute neutrality so as to get the buy-in effect of all stakeholders in the process. The success of the intervention of the DOs in local governance administration, which is based on party politics, will to a very large extent be determined by the political neutrality of the DOs because they must be seen as honest brokers in the decentralisation environment.

Again, one should be reminded that the decentralisation drive is a process and not an event. It is argued that in the future the DOs will give in to a more robust and well-capacitated local governance structure that will include the chiefdom administration, where decisions will be taken from the bottom up and not the other way round. This constitutes the real democratic, good-governance environment that all true democrats would like to see in the local governance environment in Sierra Leone, because it will be anchored on solid governance foundation, thus ensuring effectiveness, efficiency, and sustainability of the decentralisation process in Sierra Leone.

Recommendations

- The terms of reference of the DOs should be made so as not to conflict with the chief administrator in the local councils.
- That provincial secretaries and DOs should be politically neutral in their interactions with all other stakeholders in the local governance process.
- The Ministry of Local Government should ensure that each local council is treated the same as others irrespective of political ideology.
- The present intervention of the DOs should be seen as a transition phase until the local councils are adequately capacitated in the immediate future.
- The budget of the provincial secretary should be increased, and the secretary's staff should be expanded and adequately motivated to ensure effectiveness and efficiency of provincial administration.
- All stakeholders should encourage and nurture the emergence of vibrant civil society- and community-based organisations that are adequately capacitated and strengthened to act as an interface between local councils and government on the one hand and the people on the other hand.

Chapter Seven

The Role of Parliament in Strengthening the Decentralisation Process

The parliament of the Republic of Sierra Leone was instrumental in the adoption of the Local Government Act of 2004. This law facilitates the decentralization and devolution of functions, powers, and services to local councils. This chapter will examine the role of the parliament in realising the needs of the people of Sierra Leone through the decentralisation process.

In assessing the role of parliament and it functions, it is necessary to look at the 1991 constitution, particularly some of its key provisions. Sierra Leone's parliament, as the supreme legislature of the land, has a very important role to perform in the promotion and sustenance of socio-economic and political transformation in the country, and its crucial role is to ensure socio-economic transformation (i.e., improving, defending, and sustaining democratic good governance). Dominant parties in parliament must recognise that there are other legitimate interests or ideals that need to be respected and brought into negotiation over policies and not simply side-lined, attacked, or suppressed.

An attempt will also will be made to show the link between genuine political activities of parliament and parliamentarians and the promotion of socio-economic and political transformation of Sierra Leone. A parliament that is characterised by the politics of compromise based on national interest, rather than party dogma, is bound to succeed in bringing about socio-economic and political development.

The Role of Parliament in the 1991 Constitution of Sierra Leone

Section 7 of the 1991 constitution of Sierra Leone deals with the development of the economy, including harnessing Sierra Leone's natural resources in order to promote national prosperity and an efficient, dynamic, and self-reliant economy. According to the constitution, parliament is the supreme legislative body which makes laws and ensures peace, security, order, and good governance (chapter VI 73[2–3]). Parliament also has the power to regulate the finance of the state through legislations. No taxation can be imposed or raised without the authority of an act of parliament (chapter VI, section 110, part vi).

Sections 111–114 of the constitution deal with the power of parliament, which is the only arm of government that can authorise expenditure from consolidated funds or withdraw money for general revenues. Parliament can promote socio-economic transformation by ensuring transparency and accountability when it comes to state finances. For example, the auditor-general must report annually to parliament for parliamentary scrutiny (section 119[4–5]). The constitution makes parliament the supreme legislative body to which all agencies of government are accountable. Parliament remains as the principal agent for the general enforcement of democratic accountability, and it can carry out such functions through the following:

The Committee System

- Approval of government proposals; policy review
- Confirmation of executive nominees
- Authorization for taxation, appropriation, and expenditure
- Accountability for loans and gifts to the state

- Question hour
- Power for impeachment

For decades, the oversight functions of the parliament of Sierra Leone were carried out by standing committees, sessional select committees, or special select committees of the House of Parliament. The current House of Parliament of Sierra Leone (January 2014) has over thirty three committees, five of which are specialised: selection, standing orders, public petition, house, and business.

All government proposals requiring the force of law must be approved by parliament either by passing a government bill into law or by granting leave through a resolution of parliament (sections 105 and 106). It could be seen from the 1991 constitution that parliament has tremendous powers which, if used properly, will promote democratic good governance, including socio-economic transformation.

Parliament: The Bridge between the State and Civil Society

The role of parliament falls within the realm of politics aimed at mediating the respective socio-economic and political interests of the people. Parliament therefore becomes the key institutional bridge between the state and civil society. It is argued that such political activity by parliament must be carried out in ways that respect good governance, especially political openness, political participation, and political accountability.

Socio-economic transformation in Sierra Leone is inseparably linked with democratic good governance. A state can only boast of better governance when it has a developed economy which is open and therefore competitive. It is parliament that has all the powers to create an enabling environment, but to a very large extent this will depend on the strength of the parliamentary institution of the country concerned. A weak institution will lead to authoritarianism, whereas a strong one with equal partnership with the other two arms of government (the executive and the judiciary) will reign with democratic good governance. Parliament has the role to create the legal environment that will encourage the private sector to thrive. Such an environment will augur well for sustainable human development. If parliament is effective, then conflicting interests will peacefully be resolved, and broad national consensuses will forge a national development. It entails the need to be bipartisan on issues bordering on national development, as well as when voting for a bill that is put forward in parliament by the opposition. Parliamentary restrictions on voting simply because the bill is not put forward by the party under whose auspices the member of parliament was elected defeats an important ingredient of politics: compromise for national unity and development. Parochial displays of party ideologies must be discouraged, because a cold-war environment in parliament will not bode well for socio-economic transformation. Some will argue that the aforementioned restrictions constitute effective checks and balances, because it is a West Minister model, yet even the West Minister model is characterised by compromises. As a developing country, Sierra Leone should not practice partisan politics, even against the backdrop of a different socio-economic and political history. Creating enabling environments presupposes political compromises for the general good. 'Democratic politics is, rather, the politics of accommodation, compromise and the centre given a diversity of interests in society, this is inevitable. Democracy requires all-round loyalty to the democratic process itself, whatever it form and particulars. Losing parties in elections must accept the outcome and embrace the status of "loyal opposition" and they must not defect to anti-democratic forces' (Gorbridge et al. 1995, p. 433).

Socio-economic and sustainable human development will be possible where parliament has a long-term vision that focuses on the basic needs for all. The pursuit of sound macroeconomic policies to enable economic growth is required for sustainable human development. Ensuring Sierra

Leone's competitiveness domestically will reduce tariffs and make consumer goods cheaper, and ensuring a low rate of inflation complemented by budgetary policies that rule out chronic budget deficits will avoid excessive internal borrowing and facilitate gaining foreign capital. Parliament should consistently promote policies that will reduce uncertainty and institutional instability.

The above comments presuppose parliament enacting laws and also ensuring their proper implementation aimed at creating opportunities or removing obstacles for the poor, especially to ensure that the laws actually benefit the poor. In trying to bring about socio-economic transformation in Sierra Leone, parliament must first ensure the promotion of good governance. As UN Secretary-General Kofi Annan said in 1997,(Governance and Sustainable Development in Africa, UNDP, UN 28-30TH July,1997, P.1)) 'Good governance is perhaps the single most important factor in eradicating poverty and promoting development.'

Parliament and Good Governance

Parliament must ensure that it upholds democratic good governance principles, including:

- Respect for the rule of law and human rights
- Massive participation of the citizens in the decision making process
- Periodic free and fair elections
- Ensuring an independent judiciary
- Ensuring effective Service Delivery
- Ensuring accountability and transparency of public and elected officials (including the private sector) to the people who are sovereign
- Ensuring mutual tolerance

- Legislation and implementation of pro-poor policies
- Stamping out or mitigating corruption, tribalism, sectionalism, cultism, and nepotism
- Decentralization of political power
- Ensuring freedom of expression and access to information
- Maintaining a stable currency
- Minimizing dependency on donor aid
- Essential underpinning of economic and social development
- Ensuring a vibrant civil society and a private sector
- Ensuring equal opportunities for women/gender parity
- Effective civilian control over the military and other security forces

The Challenges in Post-Conflict Sierra Leone

The importance of democracy in any polity cannot be overemphasised. As Budge and Keman (1993) put it, a central democratic system is responsive to the wishes of the people and gives them the opportunity to change rulers if they so desire. This could be done through direct or indirect democracy; the latter is characterised by regular election in which the citizens can choose between competing candidates for government office. Good governance is an important component part in a democracy, and its absence will not only militate against socio-economic development but will also reduce a state to chaos and anarchy. To mitigate the possibility of such a scenario, Sierra Leone must ensure best practices in good governance characterised by the effective use of political, economic, and administrative authority.

The decentralization process in Sierra Leone, if taken very seriously and backed by the adequate political will, will soften the post-conflict socio-economic and political problems. In this regard, the parliament of Sierra Leone has a crucial role to play in the area of oversight. It must ensure not only that the provisions of the Local Government Act of 2004 are observed and implemented, but also that the necessary reforms are made aimed at strengthening the decentralisation process. Parliament must make a constant review of the document to ensure that obsolete laws and institutions that will negatively impact the work of the district councils are abolished. Parliament should also regularise the role of the paramount chiefs in the decentralisation process.

Should they play only a nominal role in the councils? Democracy in post-conflict Sierra Leone can only triumph through good governance, strengthening of efficiency and accountability of public institutions, and the promotion of political reform and stability in a balanced way. Legitimate and participative political systems and popular participation must be promoted in the political process as well as the protection of freedom of information. Parliament must also facilitate the creation of early warning systems so as to prevent or mitigate negative tendencies that are likely to impact the body politic. It will afford government the opportunity to act very swiftly in case of possible danger to the state. Parliament must ensure that a post-conflict Sierra Leone has an impartial and accessible justice system which respects human rights, supports judicial and legal reforms, and promotes justice for victims of war and violence. The justice system in Sierra Leone today is characterised by injustice. Lengthy delays mean that justice is denied to many Sierra Leoneans; this was a contributing factor for the eleven years of war in Sierra Leone.

Parliament must support economic stability and economic reform in a balanced manner, through social cohesion and economic and political participation. To avoid widening socio-economic disparities, parliament must promote equitable economic development, meet basic human needs, and reduce social exclusion by ensuring equal participation in a 'peace dividend'. Sierra Leone's natural resources must be preserved through environmental security and the creation of sustainable resource management systems, as well as support for environment rehabilitation.

Socio-culturally, parliament must give full support for constructive social dialogue and cooperation, through the promotion of culture of peace and reconciliation.

Parliament and Coalition Building

Parliament is the most strategic institution to lead the process for socio-economic and political transformation in Sierra Leone. However, parliament cannot by itself carry out the tasks of socio-economic transformation. The success of parliament in its historic task will depend on certain factors, including the nature of parliament itself. Is the atmosphere of parliament antagonistic or open to compromise? In other words, are parliamentarians ready to proffer national interest as opposed to their respective parties' interests? A parliament that is inclusive and also characterised by a national vision geared towards development will always be in a position to translate the aspirations of its people. It will also lead to the strengthening and reinforcing the credibility of parliamentarians. Parliamentarians must therefore be people characterised by nationalism, vision, pedigree, high esteem, and calibre.

Parliament should also have good relations with the executive arm of government because the latter facilitates as an implementing agency of parliament. Parliament must ensure the development of a vibrant civil society and the private sector. This is against the backdrop that parliament can legislate, but it cannot be responsible for the implementation of all its policies. It is in need of a coalition that will complement some of its activities aimed at national development. For example, one cannot overemphasise the role of the private sector in the area of job creation. Parliament must therefore strengthen ties with civil society and the private sector.

In order to enhance socio-economic and political development, parliament must also put in place mechanisms that will mitigate some of the negative aspects of globalisation. Sierra Leone has no viable option in this regard, and so parliament must ensure that its policies take into consideration globalisation trends and that its impact does not impede progress in Sierra Leone; globalisation tends to disadvantage developing countries.

If the Sierra Leone parliament is to be successful in its bid to bring about socio-economic and political development, then it must ensure massive sensitization of the Sierra Leone public. The public must be informed at all times about the politics behind the deliberations of parliament, even the adoption of certain acts of parliament.

CHAPTER EIGHT

Achievements in the Decentralisation Process

Perhaps the best success story of the decentralisation process is the gradual improvement of the mobilisation of resources. Over the years, the head tax was pegged at Le 500, but this was later increased to Le 5, 000. Many thought that the increase was going to be unacceptable to the people given the poverty that characterised the rural population. However, this belief was debunked by the positive response that the tax levy generated.

In an interview with officials in the Ministry of the then Interior, Local Government, and Community Development, now Ministry of Local Government and Rural Development it was revealed that for the past decade, local councils have not been able to raise any significant amount of tax. However, a turn-around was experienced in 2008–2009 after the government received and invested a $75,000 loan from the World Bank in order to educate the public as to the importance of the payment of head tax, the effect of which was that the local councils were able to collect over five billion Leones from the nineteen local councils in 2008–2009.

In the provincial areas of the south-east, the Bo Town council collected the highest amount of taxes, which was over Le 446 million; they were followed by Kono, with Le 420million. In the Northern Province, Koinadugu was on top with over Le 366 million, followed by Port Loko with Le 335 million. The Freetown City Council raised Le 1.485 billion. A total amount of 5.414 billion is in the respective bank accounts of the local councils. However, the ministry placed a restriction not to use the funds immediately, which led to some controversy. The said amount was increased by an additional Le. 946 million grant from government. The ministry argues that because the paramount chiefs and their officials at the chiefdom level have not been paid over the years, which in turn has led to benign neglect of the chiefdoms, some of the amount should be set aside to pay salaries to the paramount chiefs, chiefdom speakers, clerks, chiefdom policemen, messengers, and other unpaid staff. Since the beginning of 2009, 149 chiefdom officials have been paid. These chiefdoms should not exceed the following members of staff: class A chiefdoms, which are the biggest, should not have more than eight officials; class B should not have more than six; and class C should not have more than four. This is to ensure the sustainability of chiefdom administration by ensuring adequate remuneration for its officials, which will not only restore the human rights of the paramount chiefs and their officials but also motivate them to give their best in their respective assignments, thus revitalising chiefdom administration in the country.

The Sierra Leone Government in its supplementary Budget of July 2014 decided to allocate funds for the payment of Paramount Chiefs, which represents political will to improving the status of the institution of chieftaincy

To ensure transparency and accountability in the disbursement and the use of the funds, the various local councils have been requested to suggest options for the judicious use of such funds. In this regard it is argued that there should be proper monitoring to ensure that there is compliance to procurement rules characterised by a constant scrutiny of contracts, as well as full participation of the stakeholders in determining the utilisation of the funds. The fact remains that the willingness on the part of the people to pay their taxes now and in the future will, to a very large extent, depend on their judicious use, even in terms of having to show something tangible for such payments.

The local environment will be tremendously improved by ensuring that the Ward Committees function effectively and efficiently and complemented by viable civil society organisations, such as cooperatives that mobilise the people to engage in socio-economic development. The existence of such organisations remains crucial for local community development because they will complement the efforts of both government and the local councils, particularly in areas like the education of people as to what should be their proper roles and obligations towards the decentralisation process. Such organisations can also interface between the people and their local councils on the one hand and the private sector on the other hand.

When such a scenario is created, collecting the various taxes and the local community level will become much easier because the socio-economic foundations will have been laid, thus ensuring an effective, efficient, and sustainable decentralisation process for local community development. Since the inception of the decentralisation process in 2004, there are still challenges which will require both human and material resources.

Challenges of the Decentralization Process in Sierra Leone

The challenges that the decentralization process has been facing in Sierra Leone are multi-dimensional and border socio-economic and political areas.

- Unskilled human resource
- Bureaucratic hurdles
- Low revenue generation
- Donor dependency
- Inadequate subvention of local councils
- Potential conflict between local councils and paramount chiefs
- Massive illiteracy and lack of change of mind sets
- Poverty

- Gender disparity
- Inadequate infrastructure, monitoring and supervision
- Political interference and patronage
- Negative cultural practices
- Massive unemployment
- Corruption, conflecting laws, rules and regulations and procedures
- Lack of sustained political will
- Divisive, partisan politics
- Bad roads; inaccessibility of certain parts of Sierra Leone

Challenges to the Implementation of the Decentralization Programme in Sierra Leone

Although there has been rapid progress in the implementation of the decentralization programme over the years, with a lot of accomplishments in legal and regulatory areas, capacity building, and IEC, the decentralization programme has also been faced with key challenges, since its inception in 2004 in the the process to achieve its objectives. The following have been key challenges encountered in the implementation of the decentralization programme since 2004; they have been categorised under different subcomponents of the programme.

- **Strengthening policy and the implementation capacity for decentralization at a central level**

The identification of existing legislations that conflict with the decentralization policy and the provisions of the Local Government Act of 2004, as well as the compilation of those conflicting legislations, is an ongoing process and has not been completed. The existence of conflicting laws complicated the process of reviewing conflicting legislations, which was scheduled to have been completed in 2006. Substantial progress was anticipated.

It was initially extremely difficult to get the devolving ministries to fully cooperate with the Ministry of Local Government and Community Development (MILGCD) in order to ensure that functions were transferred to local councils as planned. Consequently, devolution of functions was partially carried out by the three big ministries: MEST, MOHS, and MAFFS, especially MEST. The complete transfer of functions slated by the three ministries was embarked upon in the early part of 2006. Transfer of functions by the sixteen MDAs earmarked for transfer of functions in 2006 was also facilitated. The Rapid Results Approach was used as a management tool for the acceleration of the devolution for the three big ministries that devolved functions in 2005 and was employed to fast-track the process for 2006. Additionally, capacity-building support to the devolving MDAs, to ensure that they support the devolution process and perform their oversight and monitoring functions, was a priority in 2006 however this has not been the case in 2014, the process has been very slow.

It was initially very challenging to get the local councils to establish the mandatory departments as specified in the Local Government Act of 2004. This reluctance was due mainly because of the difficulty in getting the right calibre of people in specialised local government disciplines to fill the various technical positions; there was also a lack of financial support. Since 2005, the focus had been support for the local councils in order to establish all mandatory departments and a human resource development unit. Emphasis was also directed towards the growth in numbers of professionals in these specialised areas to ensure the availability of personnel to fill the various posts in the nineteen local councils.

A related challenge was the frequent threats made by some of the local councils to get rid of their professional staff as soon as they were given the opportunity to recruit. A lot of investment had been made towards building the capacity of the present staff assigned to the councils by the central government, and dismissing staff for reasons that were unrelated to professionalism simply was a waste of resources. The LGSC was therefore supported to ensure that effective mechanisms were put in place to facilitate the retention of good staff by local councils.

The LGSC, the statutory organ responsible for regulating staffing issues at the local council level, is yet to function effectively. During the next quarter, the LGSC will be supported to establish a technical wing that will carry out specified technical functions to support the overall mandate of the LGSC.

The IMC was initially unable to meet as frequently as required, and the initial meetings were not as effective as desired due to planning issues and inadequate secretariat support. The focus therefore is to support the effective functioning of the IMC as the highest authority overseeing the implementation of the decentralization programme. Support will therefore lead towards the formal setup of the lower-level technical committee of the IMC, ensuring that the technical committee prepares the meetings for the IMC and pushes forward decisions arrived at and supporting the Decentralisation Secretariat (Dec-Sec) to function as delegated secretariat to IMC and to the sub-technical committee.

The monitoring role of the MLGCD in the decentralization programme during the initial phase of decentralisation was not effective primarily due to the lack of the requisite skills by the existing staff of the ministry, as well as the alleged lack of funds to carry out monitoring and oversight. Comprehensive training support has been provided for the MILGCD to strengthen their records management capacity. MILGCD has also been supported to establish an efficient and functional data management system.

Capacity-building support towards the strengthening of the MDAs to execute their functions under the local government system during the initial period of the decentralisation process has not been substantial. As a result, most of the MDAs were not conversant with the basic principles of decentralization and the devolution process. This gap in knowledge was bound to negatively impact the smooth transfer of functions from the MDAs to the local councils. The focus was therefore directed at providing the necessary training and coaching support for the MDAs, assisting them to integrate the RRA into the planning and implementation of their activities.

At the start of the decentralisation process, only lip service was paid to building the capacities of staff of the decentralization programme. Owing to the fact that staff were required to continuously carry out technical functions to support the implementation of the decentralization programme, there was need for continued strengthening of staff capacity to keep them updated with developments in their various professional disciplines and cope with the emerging challenges in the discharge of their duties in various disciplines and units of the programme.

- **Start-up investment and equipment in local government administrative infrastructure**

At the beginning of the decentralisation process, it was the intention of the government, through the IRCBP, to provide office space for the local councils without permanent offices within the first year of the implementation of the decentralization programme. This was not achieved as a result of the delay in procuring services of consultants and contractors, especially that of a consulting firm to support the in-house civil engineer, who needs to produce certain information such as technical and financial proposals as prescribed by the bank procurement procedures. The World Bank took a relatively longer period to review submissions. The lack of an engineering unit within the project to provide a fair spread of complementary skills among team members, and the non-existence of engineering tools such as computer-aided design (CAD) software without which the project would have to outsource some services, were also key challenges. Less reliance will be placed on external support if the issue of upgrading the engineering unit is addressed. It has been recommended that a possible way forward is to fast-track procurement procedures and to upgrade the engineering unit in terms of personnel, basic equipment, and CAD software.

- **Capacity for management and implementation of decentralised governance at local council**

According to the decentralisation secretariat, capacity building support has so far been based on a supply-driven approach. This is explained by the fact that there was limited time at the commencement of the capacity-building programme to carry out a comprehensive capacity-building needs assessment of local councils. In addition, the capacity needs of local councils and councillors were generic and almost identical; as a result, it was not possible to base capacity-building support on such assessment because the local councils needed immediate support to kick-start their activities. The focus during the initial phases of the programme was therefore to carry out a rapid needs assessment of the local councils as a basis for the provision of a broad framework of capacity-building support to the local councils. Implicitly, capacity-building support was therefore supply-driven.

At the moment, there is a gradual shift from supply-driven to a demand-driven approach, where local council actors will be encouraged to validate the needs assessment undertaken by the Regional Capacity Building Support Coordinators (RCBSCs.) which is now defunct as a result of inadequate resources.

Networking among local council actors with the view to facilitating cross-fertilization of ideas, joint planning and implementation of projects, shared learning, and experience sharing has so far not been effectively institutionalised, however it is ongoing. Emphasis is now placed on strengthening networks among local councils and promoting local council joint programme and project implementation.

Another key challenge is linked to the establishment and effective functioning of institutions below the local council level, specifically the ward committees. Most of the ward committees were not active in the initial phase of the decentralisation process because they have not been provided with the requisite support in terms of training and logistics to facilitate their effectiveness. Attention is now paid specifically to the training of the ward committees in order to ensure the acquisition of knowledge, skills, and attitudes needed to effectively perform the daunting roles and responsibilities in the decentralization programme. This is crucial if ward committees are to form an effective, efficient, and sustainable link with the local councils, thereby ensuring the participation of the grassroots in the communities.

Strengthening records management capacities of local councils – Managing records is a major area of concern in the administrative setup of most government institutions in the country, because most institutions have not cultivated the attitude of effectively managing their records and do not have the required infrastructure to support such a system. Support to local councils at the initial phase of the decentralisation process was not directed to this, and as a result most of the local councils struggled to effectively manage their records. Local councils are now supported with funding from DFID to establish viable and functioning records management systems.

- **Capacity building of local councils to design and implement infrastructure development projects**

The legal and regulatory programme was envisaged to be implemented over five years, and it will be implemented in three phases. Phase I will consist of policy writing, and of consultative and sensitization workshops with relevant stakeholders and the general public in order to inform them on the need for review. Phase II will consist of the actual review and harmonization of all laws that impact on the Local Government Act of 2004. Phase III will include sensitization of the general public of the outputs of phase II and will monitor performance. Phases I and II will be implemented through consultancy inputs to the Decentralisation Secretariat (Dec-Sec); phase III will be implemented by organizations that can receive accountable grants.

Under phases I and II, technical assistance will be provided for the following purposes.

- Strengthening of the legal and regulatory unit of Decentralisation Secretariat
- Technical assistance for the legislative review
- Drafting of the laws

In this regard, the consultants and staff of the Dec-Sec have conducted consultation workshops jointly, and NGOs have been contracted to carry out the public relations. Consultancy inputs included expatriate and legal consultants with inputs being made by officials from MLGCD, the Law Reform Commission and Law Officers Department, the Constitutional Review Committee, and other relevant stakeholders.

Phase III is housed within Dec-Sec. The staff of Dec-Sec will implement the programme through the conduct of workshops. NGOs will be contracted to carry out the public relations. The Monitoring and Evaluation (M and E) Unit within the Decentralisation Secretariat is expected to do the monitoring aspect of this phase.

- **Chiefdom governance to support and complement local council work**

The proposed programme is to be implemented in two phases over three years. Implementation of phase II will be contingent on successful implementation of phase I. Phase I will be conducted over one year and will include the development of the chiefdom policy and legislation and training for chiefs on the 2004 Local Government Act and the relationship between local councils and the chiefdom councils. Phase II will include all other activities. Phase I of the programme will be implemented through consultancy inputs to Dec-Sec and by organizations who receive that are to be accounted for. Phase II will be put out to a competitive tender. Under phase I, technical assistance will be provided for legislative review, research to inform chiefdom policy, design of the chiefdom consultations through focus group discussions, design of training modules and workshops, writing of the chiefdom policy, and drafting of the act. The consultants and staff of Dec-Sec and the MLGCD will jointly conduct the training workshops, and the initial training will be carried out at district headquarter towns. The consultants will work closely with Dec-Sec and the Law Reform Commission. NGOs will be contracted to carry out the public consultations. The consultancy inputs should include an expatriate and two local consultants.

The Chieftaincy Act of 2008 was passed by parliament and provides for the qualification, election, powers, functions, and removal of a person as a paramount chief or chief as the case may be, and for other matters connected with chieftaincy. It is expected that the act will contribute positively not only to the chiefdom administration but also to the decentralisation process as a whole.

- **Information management and communication for decentralization**

Information management within the Ministry of Interior, Local Government and Community Development (MILGCD) has been identified as one of the key weaknesses that are affecting the effective performance of the functions of the MILGCD to provide supervision and oversight under the decentralization programme. No information management or communication system is in place, making it very difficult to access information from the ministry or to ensure smooth and fast flow of information within and outside MILGCD. There are moves by the UNDP to fund a project that will come out with a communications strategy for the decentralisation scenario.

MILGCD needs support in improving its information management capabilities and flow. It is argued that government should, as a matter of priority, utilise the process of e-governance because it supports and simplifies governance for all parties: government, citizens, and businesses.

It is recommended that the government proposal to review the current information management capabilities and information flows of MILGCD and information requirements must take into cognisance the utilisation of e-governance alongside its proposal to:

- Facilitate the preparation of an information and communication strategy for MILGCD
- Support the establishment of information management unit within MLGCD
- Establish information database that will be linked to users outside MILGCD
- Develop hardware and software specifications for MILGCD databases
- Prepare guidelines for access, use, and maintenance of MILGCD databases
- Install database computers and software
- Prepare training materials and carry out in-house training in information, communication, and databases

- **IEC activities to empower stakeholders to fulfil roles and responsibilities under the decentralised system**

Creating citizen's awareness about the local government system and the decentralization programme, as well as strengthening the media to effectively promote this awareness, has been a major challenge. Designing and implementing an effective outreach programme as an integral component of the capacity building support to the decentralization programme has been a key focus of capacity-building support to the decentralization programme. The IEC unit has been strengthened to guarantee its capacity to implement the comprehensive IEC programme.

- **Strengthening national and regional service providers to train local councils**

During the initial phase of the decentralisation process, the effective identification, involvement, and assessment of service providers failed to receive the level of attention it deserved. Compounding this was the fact that tertiary institutions in the country were not well positioned or adequately suited to run the necessary courses that were required under the decentralization programme. The challenge therefore was to encourage and facilitate these institutions to expand their curriculum and design tailor-made courses that are suitable for training professionals to serve the local councils. Efforts will be directed towards facilitating the effective participation of service providers in the implementation of the decentralization programme.

Monitoring and Evaluation

Given the limited staff and resources of the IRCBP, it was able to carry out only some monitoring of the utilization of funds given to local councils and their compliance with the eligibility criteria. Monitoring of local council performance has to be intensified. The establishment of offices for the three regional capacity-building support coordinators and continued capacity building of local council coaches through training and provision of requisite logistics for their operations was given priority, and they will boost the monitoring effort.

Coordination and Collaboration with Other Partners

A major challenge has been the streamlining of capacity-building activities towards the implementation of the decentralization programme. Even though a lot of effort has been put towards the coordination of capacity-building support through the design and circulation of a comprehensive capacity-building strategy and the organization of stakeholders' workshops and meetings to consolidate efforts, the Decentralization Secretariat has not been able to streamline all the capacity-building support. Focus will continue to be directed towards the consolidation of capacity-building support in order to avoid duplication of support and over-stretching local government actors on issues of capacity building, varied approaches towards capacity building, and non-complementary support.

Despite the weaknesses and threats that characterised the decentralization scenario, Sierra Leone has both strength and opportunities which, if utilised, will contribute to a better enabling environment for the decentralisation process. These opportunities include the following:

- Potential human and material resources
- Willingness on the part of Sierra Leoneans for decentralization process
- Agricultural potential and conducive climate
- Emergence of educated paramount chiefs
- Donor goodwill and support
- Tendency toward democratic good governance and political commitment

A critical assessment and the prioritisation of the key challenges that the decentralisation process is presently facing and will continue to face perhaps revolves around youth unemployment, public service delivery, gender empowerment, and creating an enabling environment for socio-economic development of local communities, including the harmonisation of the conflict situation that characterised the relationship between the councils and the chiefdoms.

The eleven years of rebel war in Sierra Leone negatively impacted living conditions in the country. Post-conflict reconstruction efforts face immense challenges due to decades of economic mismanagement, rampant corruption, and lack of government capacity to manage the development process. The fundamental problem concerns the repackaging of the development strategies to address issues of sustained growth, poverty, and ameliorating the social and economic conditions that led to the war.

In 2008 the government of Sierra Leone reiterated that poverty is widespread in Sierra Leone and that poverty reduction remained its key objective. As such, it is also the overriding objective of this second PRSP the Agenda for Change 2008-20012 and the Agenda for Prosperity (PRSP 3) 2012-2016. It is clear from the analysis that several issues need to be addressed in order to reduce the levels of both income and non-income poverty. These issues include the following:

- Poverty is more of a rural phenomenon than an urban one, although poverty remains high in urban areas as well. Focusing on providing resources to rural areas and supporting the decentralisation process through funding and capacity building is a key to the poverty reduction process in rural areas.

- There are large variations in income poverty and non-income poverty between the different regions. Access to medical services and educational facilities vary, and significant differences in basic infrastructure such as roads exist between the regions. On average, the western region, which contains the capital city, has better indicators of population well-being than all other areas, and the northern region is the worst. Addressing the issue of regional disparities will assist in providing a more equitable distribution of resources.

- Employment is a key factor in poverty reduction. Expanding employment opportunities is central in the second and third PRSP given the large proportion of the population that is either underemployed or unemployed. Youth unemployment remains a difficult issue, particularly in urban areas; this needs to be addressed with the provision of increased education and employment opportunities in order to raise the level of economic development and reduce the possibility of social unrest.

- Educational attainment is highly correlated with income, and therefore increasing school attendance will contribute towards poverty reduction. Significant improvements have been made in school enrolment, particularly at the primary level, but secondary level attendance is still relatively low, especially for girls. This statistic suggests a need to establish measures to encourage girls to continue their education and prevent students from dropping out at secondary level.

- Access to formal employment, educational attainment, and literacy are significantly lower for women than men. In Sierra Leone women are mainly employed in agriculture. This shows the importance of gender equity throughout the implementation of the second PRSP (2008–2012).

According to the Civil Society Report for Sierra Leone (2006), Sierra Leone suffered prolonged deterioration and accompanying low standards of living. The country's economy was near collapse by the end of the 1980s, and since then it has yet to register marked increases in the growth rates of output to improve the standard of living of the majority of the Sierra Leone population. The report also stated that poverty and inflation were widespread and that most people lived on less than two dollars a day. The report further revealed that there was infrastructural deficiency, poor local capacity, and a debt burden that contributed to widespread poverty. The report stated that incomes remained very low in Sierra Leone in the public sector, and the impact on the people worsened as a result of inflation, mainly due to the recent increases in world prices for fuel and essential items, including food. The report observed that Sierra Leone had a large number of unemployed people, particularly among the youths (i.e., between fifteen and thirty-four years of age). Youth unemployment will remain a problem for the local councils for a very long period to come. The majority of Sierra Leoneans is between fifteen and thirty-four years of age. This segment of the population, according to the Sierra Leone Human Development Report (2007), is most vulnerable, and this vulnerability creates a condition for their participation in anti-social behaviour. Youth unemployment is higher at 5.2 per cent than the national rate of 3.4 per cent (Statistics Sierra Leone 2006) Youth unemployment does not augur well for peace and stability in Sierra Leone, and there is a need to put more attention and resources in youth programmes in order to immediately create jobs. The youth employment problem is affected by the fact that the private sector in Sierra Leone has not grown enough to create more decent job opportunities for the youth population.

According to the National Youth Employment Scheme Operations Manual, produced by the Ministry of Youth and Culture in July 2007, youth employment and its corollary underemployment represented a central political security issue in addition to being a socio-economic one. Youths who are able bodied but largely unskilled, jobless, and alienated are a threat to the security of the country. Addressing the physical, socio-economic, and physiological needs of youth is therefore crucial to the development of Sierra Leone. The launching of the Youth Scheme was an attempt to create an enabling environment to ensure peace and development. It merged activities related to rebuilding and increasing self-reliance and self-capacity for youths through job-creation activities in agricultural engagement, enterprise development, private sector development, and capacity building.

According to the 2004 Population and Housing Census Analytical Report of Employment and Labour Force, published in November 2006, the most popular occupation in the country was skilled agriculture, which accounted for about 37.9 per cent of the occupation of the cash-earning population; a slightly higher percentage of females (39.5 per cent) than males (36.5 per cent) were cash earners engaged in agriculture.

An occupational distribution of labour force (fifteen to sixty-four years) by sex depicts that about 88.3 per cent of the total labour force is in low-skilled occupation such as service workers, shop and market sales workers, and agriculture and fishing workers. There are more females (93.7 per cent) than males (83.0 per cent) engaged in economic activities in all age groups in Sierra Leone. Activities in the informal sector are also dominated by women. Women in Sierra Leone are engaged in paid employment in education (25.7 per cent, as opposed to 19.4 per cent for males) and agriculture (14.2 per cent as opposed to 11 per cent) (Population and Housing Census Sierra Leone 2006). At the universities, women constituted less than 20 per cent. In all, women were under-represented in political, economic, and educational contexts in Sierra Leone.

The way forward in a decentralised Sierra Leone is multi-faceted. First of all, an evaluation of the transition process must be carried out, and the necessary reforms should be made. There should be no turning back in the effort to strengthen democratic good governance in Sierra Leone. This must be complemented by the cooperation of all stakeholders, particularly the political parties, the donor community, and the Sierra Leone public. As a multi-ethnic society, Sierra Leoneans must ensure that the decentralization process is non-partisan.

Efforts should be made for more women and youth to be adequately represented, even if by a quota system. Chiefdom governance must be carried out vigorously through the development of economic development based on the comparative advantage of regions. The private sector should be encouraged to invest in the regions complemented by government, creating an enabling environment such as unimpeded access to land and tax holidays. The autonomy of the councils must be protected; the ruling class at any given time must avoid interfering in the politics of local government.

Decentralization in Sierra Leone must be seen as an investment in social change. Institutions and structures must be complemented by competent staff to ensure that these institutions that are crucial to the overall success of the decentralization process are managed efficiently, effectively, and sustainably.

Chiefdom Governance

Despite current attempts at reforming chiefdom administration, Sierra Leone's 149 chiefdoms are, to a very large extent, not properly organised and lack good governance as well as basic amenities, crucial institutions, and structures that can positively complement the district councils in their bid for socio-economic development. The majority of the people in rural areas are very poor, and chiefdoms have been highly dependent on government grants. The move by the government to impose a temporary ban on the use of funds is to ensure that the chiefdoms are transparent and accountable. The present action on the part of the government to bring about chiefdom reform is a move in the right direction. Parliament adopted a 2009 Chieftaincy Act in parliament to regulate the qualification, election, powers, functions, and removal of a person as a paramount chief. The core of this reform should find a place for the paramount chief's by integrating that institution into the governance process; this will go a very long way to giving it something to play with, rather than it becoming spoilers to the governance system.

Since the decentralisation process started, the chiefdoms have not felt the positive impact of the process. For the chiefdoms, the present decentralisation drive is viewed as 'decentralised, but centralised' because although the national government has devolved some of its powers, functions, and services to the districts councils, the chiefdoms were not given any defined role in the Local Government Act of 2004. Since 2009 serious attempts have been made to empower the chiefdom administration, such as the payment of officials of chiefdom administration after over a decade of neglect. Government has also installed all the 288 court chairmen in all the chiefdoms, and with the payment of salary. The National Electoral Commission conducted chieftaincy elections to fill over 38 paramount chief vacancies; these appointments and more are aimed at bringing about better governance and socio-economic development at the chiefdom level. This tactic will no doubt minimise the tendency on the part of the paramount chiefs to treat their chiefdoms as personal fiefdoms, and they will also start to see themselves as custodians of the rights of their people.

Vigorous attempts at creating civil society organisations and cooperatives that bring about increased production, economic activity, and thus surplus should be made. This will boost both intra- and international trade; however it requires a good infrastructure. The development of cooperatives would contribute to the emergence of a vibrant, community-based civil society and private sector organisations. Cooperatives must also be fully complemented by mechanised farming, funding, and access to seedlings and fertiliser. The creation of economically viable entities will increase the income or revenue of the respective chiefdoms and will create not only the payment of taxes but also a firm basis for socio-economic development.

Another problem that characterised the chiefdoms is that villages are far apart, which makes it very difficult (if not impossible) to provide amenities that should benefit a larger community. It is argued that bringing the villages together would have been a viable option. For now, however, this problem will be mitigated primarily by road networks, junior and senior secondary schools, and hospitals with adequate staff.

The Comprehensive Local Government Performance Assessment System

In 2006, two years after the decentralisation process started, the Comprehensive Local Governance Performance Assessment System (CLoGPAS) was carried out. The decentralization policy stipulated the period 2004–2008 as a transitional period. The local councils were already past mid-term since its inception in 2004. It was expedient that a period of review focused on ascertaining the level of performances of the local councils be undertaken to determine the relationship between efforts at capacity building undertaken during the period, the resource flow and fiscal transfers to the councils, and the output in terms of services and development to and within communities.

CLoGPAS found that no council met the six minimum conditions: financial management; functional capacity in development planning;

functional capacity and accountability; functional capacity in procurement, transparency, and accountability; project implementation; and local council functional capacity. Institutions in Sierra Leone have always been plagued by financial impropriety, which often leads to their demise. To meet this challenge, the Local Government Act of 2004 requires local councils to prepare proper books of accounts, prepare financial statements, and present accounts to external auditors (the office of the auditor). Thus, meeting this minimum condition in financial management remains crucial and requires councils to manage funds, submit accounts to external auditors as stipulated in the Local Government Act and other regulations, and receive 'unqualified' opinion from the auditors.

Development planning has and still is the key instrument for rapid socio-economic transformation of most societies and institutions. In this light, during their two years of existence, local councils have been able to prepare development plans that prioritise their needs and the way they want to see their communities in the future. However, it has become very useful to determine local councils' compliance with the development planning guidelines and plan implementation. Thus local councils must fulfil the following in order to meet the minimum conditions for functional capacity in development planning:

- Preparation of the development plan in compliance with the MoDEP (now the Ministry of Finance) or LGFD/DECSEC planning guidelines
- Consultations with the general population, communities, and NGOs in the preparation of the plan
- Availability of the plan to the general public

Fiscal and financial discipline, or the lack of it, has been a stumbling block in the implementation of development programmes in Sierra Leone. As a result, institutions have always been plagued with financial impropriety, which often leads to their demise. It could be recalled that local councils were abolished mainly because of financial malpractices. Therefore an assessment of local councils in functional capacity in budgeting and accounting will ensure fiscal discipline and encourage popular participation and increase public confidence. Local councils must fulfil all of the following to meet the minimum condition for budgeting and accounting:

- Budget preparation, consideration and approval by the local council, and submission to the Local Government Finance Committee three months before the beginning of the financial year
- Ensuring a balance between incomes and expenditures, and inclusion of the projects planned to be undertaken in the development plan
- Preparation of the annual statement of accounts within the first quarter of a succeeding budget

The country is going through a lot of institutional reform processes, including governance and procurement as a global requirement. The local councils are also part of the local governance reform structure and are required to adhere to the reform in the procurement process. Meeting the functional capacity in procurement requires council to meet the following indicators:

- Full establishment and constitution of the local council's procurement committee
- Composition of the procurement committee in accordance with the NPPA and the 2004 Local Government Act
- A properly constituted procurement committee should meet before, during, and after the procurement process

- Possession of the Public Procurement Act of 2004 and Public Procurement Guidelines (2006)
- Council's procurement plan has been updated in the last six months
- Council's procurements are undertaken in accordance with the updated and approved procurement

The fulfilment of transparency requirements in the Local Government Act of 2004 is central to the implementation of the decentralization programme. Hitherto, the business of institutions was shrouded in secrecy, which made them vulnerable to corruption and prevented the public from gaining confidence in them. The minimum condition for transparency and accountability assesses the local council's compliance with the provisions of section 107 of the Local Government Act of 2004 and specifically deals with the posting of the following public documents:

- Monthly statements of financial accounts
- Annual income and expenditure statements (annual accounts)
- Inventories of assets of the local councils
- Minutes of council meetings
- The development plan

The following indicators are included
Preparation, approval, and submission of an acceptable project profile

- Did the council prepare a project brief and profile for the current fiscal year?
- Were the approved project briefs and profiles submitted to LGFD/DECSEC three months before the start of financial year 2006?
- What were the reasons why they were not submitted within the stipulated timeframe?
- Submission of progress reports on project implementation

- Did the council submit financial and physical progress reports to LGFD for all projects in 2005?
- Were the progress reports deemed acceptable by IRCBP?

The Local Government Act of 2004 made provisions for local councils to convene and conduct monthly council meetings in order to discuss and make decisions on matters relevant to the localities' welfare. Councils must have held at least one meeting per month for the last twelve months to meet this minimum condition.

Councils are assessed on the following indicators for this performance measure:

- Establishment of subcommittees
- Establishment of ward committees
- Adoption and use of the standing orders
- Establishment and work of the mandatory departments

According to the report, the three councils that met the most minimum conditions (Kailahun District, Bo District, and Kambia District) failed to meet *all* the minimum conditions on account of their failure to meet the two earlier mentioned indicators, such as the establishment of the sub and ward committees respectively.

The report added that the best performance on the performance measures was the Kono District Council, which passed 83 per cent of the indicators. Bonthe district, which registered the second-best score, passed 82 per cent of the indicators. Eleven councils passed more than 70 per cent of the indicators. The report stated that only one council, Western Area Rural, passed less than 50 per cent of the performance measures indicators.

According to the report, there are two factors responsible for the inability of councils to meet indicators for some of the minimum conditions and performance measures: those factors internal to the local councils themselves, and those that emanate from the failure of MDAs to provide required support to the councils. It is noted that most of the factors internal to the councils themselves were due to two main challenges: lack of trained staff or resources to carry out the functions required to meet the minimum conditions, and performance measures. The report observed that some councils lacked staff with the skills to prepare accounts and budgets for timely submission to such bodies as the auditor general or LGFD. Lack of competent staff was also responsible for the inability of councils to conduct valuation exercises, establish and run the mandatory committees, or conduct monitoring and evaluation exercises.

Factors emanating from MDAs were due to the low priority given by top-level decisions makers in the MDAs to the overall decentralization process. Top-level decision making and coordinating bodies for the decentralization process (IMC & PCC) were not doing enough to address emerging urgent, critical, and overarching challenges facing the decentralization process and local councils. These challenges, the report went on, included breach of procurement, tensions between administrative and political leadership of councils, constraints on own revenue mobilization by councils, cases of inactivity from certain MDAs to support the devolution process, delay in fiscal transfer of funds from central government to local councils, and failure of the office of the auditor general to present audit reports to the local councils. The report emphasised that decentralization also requires MDAs to take on additional functions, at least in the short run. Many of these MDAs, however, did not have the capacity, staff, and resources to perform these additional functions. For instance, whilst devolution requires MDAs to devolve some their functions, assets, and personnel, the actual process of devolution itself requires documentation, verification, and other activities related to huge-scale transfers, and many MDAs did not have the personnel or the capacity to perform. The report stated that the devolution exercise also meant additional functions for the local councils, and most of them did not have the capacity to absorb these functions or verify, take possession of, and utilise devolved assets and personnel.

According to the report on the findings of the MDAs, the Inter Ministerial Committee (IMC) did not meet as regularly as prescribed in the Local Government Act of 2004 and did not develop procedures to regulate its meetings. It had not develop a framework and guidelines on delegation of powers and functions. It also did not have a functioning coordinating secretariat. This constituted a big challenge to the process that was designed to address emerging urgent, critical, and overarching challenges facing the decentralization process and local councils, such as breach of procurement, tensions between administrative and political leadership of councils, own revenue mobilization by councils that were linked to lack of cooperation by traditional authorities, addressing cases of inactivity from certain MDAs to support the devolution process, and delays in fiscal transfer of funds from central government to local councils.

The lack of a dedicated coordinating secretariat for the IMC also undermined effective pre-meetings preparation as well as the establishment of focused mechanisms to track and follow up on decisions of the IMC.

CLoGPAS also identified the failure on the part of the provincial coordinating committees (PCC) to meet quarterly as required by the Local Government Act of 2004.

Despite the fact that the office of the auditor general had formulated relevant polices to support the decentralization process and had in place a focal point for decentralization, the focal point did not receive relevant support from other MDAs.

The office audited council accounts for the 2004 financial year. The local councils did not present these accounts to the auditors within the first three months of 2005, as required by the Local Government Act; most were presented in September 2005. No audit reports had been presented by the office of the auditor general at the time of the assessment to the local councils in 2006.

In 2006 the Ministry of Interior, Local Government and Community Development had not prepared guidelines and sensitised local councils on the distribution of locally generated revenue and also guidelines on investments by local councils. It was only in 2008 that the government gave chiefdoms the right to utilise the revenue collected by them and the opening of a bank account by the respective chiefdoms.

Both the MILGCD and the DECSEC supported the design of a monitoring system and facilitated the recruitment and training of M&E officers in the local councils. The report stated that emphasis had been placed on active community participation during the implementation of community-driven projects, and both institutions had also ensured civil society participation in devolution workshops and encouraged councils to have open budget days.

On the implementation of the Local Government Act, both the local government and the Decentralization Secretariat developed guidelines for preparation of statutory instruments and had a mechanism for reviewing these instruments.

According to the CLoGPAS, the Local Council Finance Committee (LGFC), the Local Government Finance Department, and the Ministry of Finance had been established and were fully constituted. It formulated the relevant policies to support the decentralization process. The report observed that the Local Government Act was weak on setting criteria for representation in the LGFC; thus most members of the LGFC lacked the technical expertise to provide effective oversight.

On the issue of grants to local councils, the LGFD had also designed a grant distribution formula and sensitised local councils on this formula. LGFD grant allocations reflected local council expenditure needs and revenue capacity. There had been increases in total grants allocation to local councils in compliance with the law and to reflect the proportion of functions devolved to the councils. No council had appealed against the grant allocation formula.

The LGFD had a framework for monitoring the local councils and had conducted monitoring exercises on the (tied grant) financial resources of councils. The report observed that although payments to the councils were made on a quarterly basis, the amount paid to councils was not equal to the annual allocated amounts. This was in part due to resource constraints at the central government level.

Despite the existence of a grant disbursement schedule, this was not adhered to by the Ministry of Finance due to central government resource limitations. Conditions for the receipt of grants by local councils were also not strictly adhered to. The lack of strict adherence was due to the fact that funds started flowing to the local councils very late.

Conclusion

For any nation to achieve socio-economic development, its foundations have to be built on democratic good governance. Parliament cannot actualise its national agenda alone; it must therefore endeavour to ensure the strengthening of democratic good governance as the foundation for socio-economic and political development, as well as forge partnerships with civil society and the private sector. It must also establish a legal and regulatory framework to ensure stability and equity in the application of laws and regulations; this will ensure an environment that is conducive for socio-economic and political development, reduces corruption, and encourages savings and investments.

Parliament must keep opposing interests in equilibrium; this will strengthen both parliament and society. The capacity of parliament to enact laws and resolve conflicts between various social groups should be further strengthened, especially because Sierra Leone is a multi-ethnic society in need of long-term peace to ensure positive development. An effective overall parliamentary monitoring mechanism can ensure the effective, efficient, transparent, accountable, and equitable functioning of the three branches of government.

The decentralisation process of 2004–2014 is badly in need of reform. More effort should be made to enlarge the sources of revenue on the part of both the councils and government, because the bottom line of any successful decentralisation process is the availability of human and material resources.

Another area that government should intensify is the adoption and utilisation of e-governance to enhance the local government process and reduce costs. E-governance can support and simplify governance for government, citizens, and businesses. With a comprehensive communication strategy, the government will be able to provide citizens access to information and knowledge about the political process, services, and the choices available. Both the external and internal strategic objectives of e-governance should be aimed at satisfying the needs and expectations of the public, and ensuring the facilitation of government operations to ensure a speedy, transparent, accountable, efficient, and effective process for performing government administration activities. However, the necessary institutions and structures that will radically enhance the information process all over the country are yet to be put in place. There is a need for the government to encourage more investment from other partners because the government cannot provide the necessary funding to ensure a significant transformation in the area of the use of ICTs for effective, efficient, and sustainable local governance in Sierra Leone.

Decentralisation and local governance is a process that is continuous, and therefore it is not an event that will be experienced or celebrated for a moment. The process will be characterised by several phases, none of which will be final. Each phase is determined by the conscious and guided activities of all the stakeholders (government, citizens, local councils, NGOs, community-based and private sector organisations, and the donor community). These stakeholders need to work together to achieve the objective of decentralisation and local governance. Moving forward will at times be very difficult, but one must not relent so as to not be relegated to the backyard of history. We must reckon with history, or else we stand to be condemned by it.

A decade since the inception of the decentralisation process, local governance is gradually taking shape, yet much more effort is to be made to harmonise the conflict situation that exist between the 19 councils on the one hand and the 149 chiefdoms on the other hand. Despite modest gains, numerous challenges still remains in key areas. Perhaps the most important challenge is in the area of councils not receiving adequate resources to facilitate the decentralisation process, and budgetary allocations have not been made for some functions. This is against the backdrop that international funding came to an end when the World Bank project that facilitated the decentralisation process came to an end. Since then, the decentralisation process had to be fully subvented by the government. The situation has been further aggravated as a result of late submission of quarterly financial and technical reports by the councils to facilitate timely disbursement of funds by the Ministry of Finance.

In the case of the devolution process since 2004, the eighty functions were slated to be devolved to councils by the end of 2008, but only thirty-two were devolved by December 2008. Since then twenty-four more functions have been devolved, although some only partially. Sixteen MDAs were to devolve various functions and activities to local councils, but only nine MDAs have devolved functions by 2014.

Another area is that of building the capacities of the local councils; this should include strengthening the capacities of the MDAs to perform their residual functions of policy setting, standards setting, quality assurance, capacity building, and monitoring and evaluation.

Devolution of personnel were available, and MDAs have transferred those staff to the local councils, but in a de-concentrated fashion characterised by personnel still receiving their salaries from their parent departments. Such a development had led to a psyche of alienation where personnel have not been regarded as staff of the respective councils compared to the core staff that they have recruited. Local councils have not been involved in the assignment of their staff. There had been instances of unwillingness by the MDAs to cooperate by using bureaucratic means to either prevent or delay the transfer of personnel to local councils.

This is against the backdrop that some functions required to be transferred to local councils are highly technical, and the devolving MDAs lack the personnel and resources. There has been also a tendency for most MDAs to not have a database on inventory of assets and personnel, even where available. In some instances they have been reluctant to pass on the information.

The decentralization process will continue to face major challenges because there is a tendency for the MDA's failure to be proactive because of the lack of a change of mindset and political will. There is a failure on the part of many government officials to accept the devolution process. In this regard there should be public education aimed at making government officials, including government ministers, professional heads, and politicians on the devolution process, have adequate understanding of the decentralization process. The government should continue to demonstrate strong political will in support of the ongoing decentralization programme.

The legal environment of the decentralization process is characterised by conflicts of laws, rules, regulations, and procedures. There will be a need to harmonise the laws that characterised the local governance environment, which will help promote the decentralisation process. It has been argued that since the decentralisation process started, monitoring and supervision has been poor from the central government. For example, the taskforce should be set up to continually engage those MDAs that have not devolved.

A very crucial aspect of decentralization is perhaps the status of it driver the councillors and the Word Committees who do not have fixed salaries that will help to sustain their motivation. It is argued that government should consider this aspect if the decentralization process is to gain further momentum.

The decentralization process will receive the blessings of the 1991 revised constitution when it would have been put together by the Constitutional Review Committee set up by the government in July 2013. The original 1991 constitution did not have any provisions on local government architecture in Sierra Leone since it came in being in 2004. It is hoped that some of the contradictions that characterised the local governance environment such as that existing between the councils and the chiefdoms will be solved or mitigated.

Bibliography

Abraham, A. *Paramount Chieftaincy and Its Post Conflict Role in Sierra Leone.* Virginia State University: Burke Perry & Dellinger, 2003.

'Agenda for Change: Second Poverty Reduction Strategy (PRSP 11) 2008–12'. Freetown: Government of Sierra Leone, 2008.

Alie, J. A. D. *A New History of Sierra Leone.* London: Macmillan Publishers, 1990.

'Anti-Corruption Act of 2008'. Supplement to the *Sierra Leone Gazette,* Vol. cxxxix, no. 45 (18 September 2008). Freetown: Government Printers.

Annan Kofi. Governanceand Sustainable Development in Africa, UNDP, UN 28-30 July 1997.

Auclair, C. *Federalism: Its Principles, Flexibility and Limitations.* Paper presented at the International Conference on Decentralisation. Manila, Philippines, 2002.

Bahl, R. W. and Linn, J. F. 'The Assessment of Local Government Revenues.' In *Developing Countries,* edited by Charles E. McLure, Jr. Canberra: Centre for Research on Federal Finance Relations, Australian National University, 1983.

Bahl, R. W. and Linn, J. F. *Urban Public Finance in Developing Countries.* New York: Oxford University Press, 1992.

Brima, J., Samuel, P. S., Amara. Kargbo, B., and Moseray, B. *2004 Population and Housing Census: Analysis Report on Employment and Labour Force Statistics*. Sierra Leone, 2006.

Brown, M. 'Governance: A Bedrock of Development'. *Choices Magazine*. New York: UNDP, 1999.

Budge I. and Keman, H. *Parties and Democracy: Coalition Formation and Government Function in Twenty States*. New York: Oxford University Press, 1993.

Cheema, G. Shabbir. *Choices Magazine*. New York: UNDP, 1998.

'Chieftaincy Act of 2008'. Freetown: Government Printers Freetown Supplement to the Sierra Leone Gazette Volcxxxix. No.50 dated 16 october2009

CIVICUS. *Civil Society Index Report for the Republic of Sierra Leone: A Critical Theme of Civil Society in Sierra Leone, Campaign for Good Governance and Christian Aid*. Sierra Leone, 2006.

Corbridge, S. and Barrow, C. *New Directions in Development Studies*. Great Britain: Arnold Publication, 1995.

Litvack. Jennie, et. al Rethinking Decentralisation in Develop0ing Countries, World Bank, Washington DC. 1998.

'Local Government Act of 2004'. Printed as a supplement to the *Sierra Leone Gazette* Vol. cxxxv, no. 15 (4 March 2004). Freetown: Government Printers.

Ministry of Local Government and Rural Development, National Devolution Workshop 1–4 July 2013. Draft Final Report. Freetown, 2013.

Ministry of Youth and Culture. *National Youth Employment Scheme Operations Manual.* Freetown.

'The 1991 Constitution of Sierra Leone.' Printed as a supplement to the *Sierra Leone Gazette Extraordinary,* Vol. cxxii. no. 59 (25 September 2000). Freetown: Government Printers 2000.

Presidential Address, State Opening of Parliament 2008 and 2013, Parliament Building, Tower Hill, Freetown. 2008 and 2009.

'Public Procurement Act of 2004'. Printed as a supplement to the *Sierra Leone Gazette* Vol. cxxxv, no. 70 (16 December 2005). Freetown: Government Printers.

Rondinelli, D. A., Nellis J. R., and Cheema, G. S. *Planning and Realisation of Projects in Development,* volume 5. Beverley Hills: Sage, 1984.

Suma Mohamed, Rule of Law:A Review by AfiMAP and Open Society Initiative for West Africa, Freetoen, January 2014.

Sierra Leone Governance Round Table Report on Local Government and Decentralisation. Freetown, Sierra Leone: UNDP, 2002.

Sierra Leone Human Development Index Report. Freetown: UNDP, 2007.

Statement on the Supplementary Government Budget for the Financial Year 2014-09-04 10TH July 2014, Government Printing Department, Freetown 2014.

Stockmayer, A. 'Decentralisation and Poverty Reduction'. *Policy Insight,* no.5. OECD Development Centre, 1999.

Task Force on Decentralisation and Local Governance, District Level Consultations Final Report, GOSL/UNDP/DFID. Freetown, 2003.

Tendler, J. *Good Government in Topics.* Baltimore: Johns Hopkins University Press, Asian Development Bank Review, 1995.

Ward Committee Facilitators Training Manual for Councils in Sierra Leone, GOSL, Ministry of Local Government, Freetown 2011.

www.ingramcontent.com/pod-product-compliance
Lightning Source LLC
Chambersburg PA
CBHW020520290526
45786CB00002B/686